DIRTY STOP OUT'S GUIDE to 1980s SHEFFIELD
★ by Neil Anderson ★

Published by
★ACM ЯETRO

Classic Cinema in Fitzalan Square

Copyright © 2011 Neil Anderson

All rights reserved. No part of this book may be reproduced in any form or by any electronic or mechanical means, including information storage or retrieval systems, without permission in writing from the publisher, except by a reviewer who may quote brief passages.
Every effort has been made to trace the copyright holders of photographs in this book but one or two were unreachable.
We would be grateful if the photographers concerned would contact us.

Published by ACM Retro Ltd,
The Grange,
Church Street,
Dronfield,
Sheffield S18 1QB.

ISBN: 978-1-908431-06-6

Visit ACM Retro at: www.acmretro.com

Neil Anderson asserts the moral right to be identified
as the author of this work.
A catalogue record for this book is available from the British Library.

*Front cover shot: 'The Only Way Is Up' -
demand for Insette Extra Hold hairspray was unprecedented in the 1980s.*

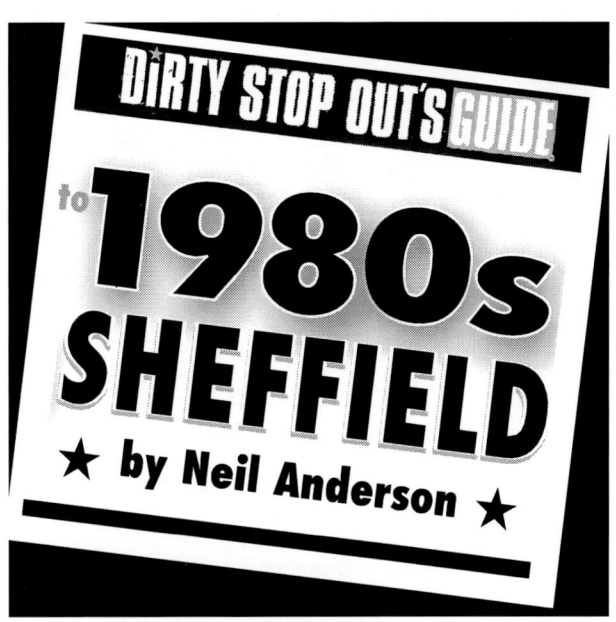

DiRTY STOP OUT'S GUIDE to 1980s SHEFFIELD
★ by Neil Anderson ★

Published by
★ACM ЯETRO

The dark days of the bitter Miners' Strike - police march from Campo Lane to Vicar Lane

Busking outside the Underground on Charles Street

CONTENTS

● Introduction - Electro-pop revolution rescues decade of nightmares — P9

Chapter 1 — P13
● Eat, drink and be merry - for tomorrow the redundancy runs out

Chapter 2 — P19
● Josie's - the champagne king of 1980s clubbing

Chapter 3 — P27
● 'Rock On The Rates' with The Leadmill

Chapter 4 — P37
● Rebels, rockers and total 'Hysteria'

Chapter 5 — P43
● 'Is that all right for youse?' - enter The Roxy

Chapter 6 — P51
● Rock'n'roll is alive and well... And living on Staniforth Road

Chapter 7 — P57
● All-conquering League paves the way for Steel City chart success

Chapter 8 — P63
● Limit's Lyceum gamble brings gig heaven to Sheffield

Chapter 9 — P67
● Roger & Out and punk night at The Marples

Chapter 10 — P71
● Rebina and X Clothes - how to sign on in style

Chapter 11 — P75
● Paula Yates bombs at Radio Rentals and other '80s quirks

Chapter 12 — P79
● Jive Turkey - the coolest club in the country?

DiRTY STOP OUT'S GUIDE to 1980s SHEFFIELD

The old Cannon Cinema on Flat Street (formerly Cinecenta)

The aftermath of Def Leppard drummer Rick Allen's devastating car crash on New Year's Eve, 1984, that severed his left arm

Colley Working Mens' Club

Lizzy and Natalie of Myers Tripe Stall

DiRTY STOP OUT'S GUIDE to 1980s SHEFFIELD

The Limit and the legendary chip shop next door on West Street

The Popular Bee Hive

DiRTY STOP OUT'S GUIDE to 1980s SHEFFIELD

ELECTRO-POP REVOLUTION RESCUES DECADE OF NIGHTMARES

Left: All-conquering Human League of the 1980s

1981 was the year when a new breed of Sheffield music truly arrived. Not nationally, but globally.

The seventies had been a bit of chart disaster; bar Tony Christie we'd hardly bothered the UK top twenty.

But the eighties were our calling, our Ground Zero, our aural assault and then some.

Steel City was about to become electro-pop-Mega-City-One and the Human League's 1981 'Dare' album was the genre defining long-player that took the city's musical career stratospheric.

● **The eighties were our calling, our Ground Zero, our aural assault and then some.**

Released in October of that year, it took the world by storm and paved the way for 'Don't You Want Me', the December single that hit the top spot both here and in the USA.

The region didn't need asking twice - Heaven 17, ABC, Cabaret Voltaire, Clock DVA, Comsat Angels, Artery, Vision, Pulp, Danse Society and scores of other local acts lined up for a piece of the action.

It was a good job really, we needed a distraction. Other than entertainment the decade was the stuff of nightmares.

Under Thatcher's watch there was one proper war (the Falklands) which helped her landslide victory in 1983; a near civil war at the hands of the Miners' Strike which first started in South Yorkshire at Cortonwood Colliery; mass unemployment and Armageddon looking a near given with a worsening of US/Russian relations in the continuing Cold War.

No leader of the 20th century outside of wartime ever held anything like the psychological grip Thatcher held over its people.

Some went to extreme lengths to get release - the suicide rate apparently doubled every time she won a new term in office.

Like her or loathe her, she permeated parts of society previously untouched by a Prime Minister.

Her pervading views of the free market economy and patriotism couldn't have been more at odds with the new left who were preaching anti-racism, anti-war, anti-sexism with the help of a new strain of alternative comedians, Red Wedge Tours with the likes of Paul Weller and Billy Bragg enlisted to try and bolster the Labour vote and CND rallies.

Sheffield didn't take things lying down in the area soon to be referred to as the 'People's Republic of South Yorkshire'. The city was declared a 'nuclear free zone,' the red flag flew over the Town Hall and free gigs were held for UB40 holders.

Ready for action at Josephine's

DiRTY STOP OUT'S GUIDE to 1980s SHEFFIELD

We welcomed the filming of Barry Hines's 'Threads' (1984) - the documentary-style film that showed Sheffield in the build up and aftermath of a nuclear attack. Though it definitely got the point across, it left an entire generation traumatised...

If politics weren't your thing or you simply wanted to drink yourself to oblivion after watching the mushroom cloud rising over the city you could lose yourself in the champagne bar at Josephine's, wander the cavernous Romeo and Juliet's (later to become Cairo Jax) on Bank Street or climb the hallowed stairs to Isabella's on Eyre Street.

If you fancied a surreal day time distraction you could always try the mighty' 'Bendy Bus'. The unfeasibly long mode of transport was a bizarre hit. And even if your particular bus didn't bend, it probably still happily ran all night with an average fare of next to nothing (which was the scheme of things in this decade of heavily subsidised bus fares).

Above: The Stonehouse

> "Where there is discord, may we bring harmony."
> — Margaret Thatcher

Things didn't fare so well for the once mighty 'Hole in the Road'. Winos aside, the subterranean institution was fast falling out of favour as the escalators ground to a halt and the graffiti artists moved in to redecorate.

Subtle wasn't a phrase you'd use to describe 1980s Sheffield. It was bold, brutal and outlandish - and that was just the crimped hair ascending the stairs at the West Street dole office.

It was the era of youth culture in turmoil with factions rising and falling at an alarming rate: trendies; Goths; psychobillys; second wave punk merchants; vege-charged anarchists; Greenham Common feminists; acid house; metal; scooter boys; skinheads; new romantics; yuppies and more.

Sales of Dr Marten footwear were at an all time high as everyone, bar the vegans, seemed to adopt them; 'Flashdance' (1983) gave us legwarmers and American cheerleaders can be blamed for 'ra ra' skirts that swept the nation.

Sheffield's own Phil Oakey had a lot to answer for. As well as dictating the nation's listening tastes, he also pioneered the kind of asymmetric haircut that became symbolic of the decade.

If we didn't like the music there was always football. The trophy cabinets might have been pretty barren landscapes for both home teams in the eighties but inter-fan rivalry was at an all time high as the police struggled to contain the pitched battles between local firms.

The 1989 Hillsborough Disaster scars run deep to this day whilst Heysel happened in Europe.

Though we all liked the alternative edge of Sheffield's X Clothes and Rebina shoes on the shopping front, we were all secretly relieved Redgates was still flying the flag for toys.
In a decade devoid of bars with late licences it was up to the clubs to provide the dance floors whilst the pubs provided the alcohol-charged rocket fuel to get you in groove mode: Pig & Whistle, the Stonehouse, the Old Blue Bell, Henry's, the Marples, Hanrahans, the Golden Ball, the Geisha Bar (later to become Legends), the Frog & Parrot, West Street's Hallamshire, Mailcoach and Beehive, and so, so many more provided the pre-nightclub entertainment!

Welcome ladies and gents, to the 'Dirty Stop Out's Guide to 1980s Sheffield'.

The Roxy

Park Hill flats

EAT, DRINK AND BE MERRY - FOR TOMORROW THE REDUNDANCY RUNS OUT

Nightlife didn't exactly have the most auspicious start to the 1980s in Sheffield.

Though we were lining up for an era defined by big hair, bigger shoulder pads and all round 'urban tough' fashion-charged attitude; it wasn't quite so easy when you realised you'd got little more than a UB40 to fund this brave new MTV-inspired world.

The recession was biting deep into Sheffield's industrial heartland in the early eighties and club land was one of the first areas to feel the knock on effects of fast depleting disposable incomes.

Though the 1970s were hardly an era of sweetness and light, we were pretty much at the top of our game by the time the legendary 1971 flick 'Sheffield City On The Move', the film that ended up appearing as part of 'The Full Monty' years later, appeared.

● *It wasn't quite so easy when you realised you'd got little more than a UB40 to fund this brave new MTV-inspired world*

We boasted the 'biggest nightclub in Europe' in the shape of the Fiesta; the sprawling Top Rank next door was lining up to stage gigs from groundbreaking acts spanning Bowie to Magazine in the coming years and we seemed to have more bars, pubs, wine bars and Working Men's Clubs than ever before.

Roll on a decade or so and the death knell was being sounded on much of the scene in 1983.

A weather-beaten 'For Sale' sign hung optimistically outside the Fiesta - a venue that had now been empty three years.

Five separate organisations - including Norton Entertainments who had first launched it with a massive fanfare in the summer of 1970 - had tried and sadly failed to make a go of the 24,500 square foot cabaret club that arguably came closer than any UK venue in landing a gig by Elvis Presley.

It was the city's great white hope that helped make a star of Sheffield's own Marti Caine and brought everyone from the Jacksons to Stevie Wonder to Arundel Gate.

The last management operation to try and make a go of it called it a day after eight months with debts reported at more than half a million pounds.

The story wasn't much more encouraging next door at the Top Rank which was also up for sale. There'd been no takers.

Left: Pinstone Street

Looking down Fargate

DiRTY STOP OUT'S GUIDE to 1980s SHEFFIELD

DING DONG EVERYTHING WENT WRONG

It wasn't just mainstream venues that were suffering in 1983. Live music venue Dingwalls closed its Eyre Street doors after just six months.

Gig-goers thought all their birthdays had come at once when the venue, as part of a nationwide roll-out programme, first opened in Sheffield.

The acts came thick and fast on a nightly basis. Rock, indie, punk - no music genre was off limits.

It's not as if the city was doing that badly on the live music front at that point. The Leadmill was firing on all cylinders, The Limit was fighting fit and Sheffield Polytechnic's Nelson Mandela building was bringing up the rear with Sheffield City Hall and others.

Dingwalls manager Martin Baird blamed the bands for charging too much which meant the admission price became too much for punters to pay.

He apparently tried smaller names but nobody turned up.

His outlook on the scene he was bowing out of was hardly uplifting:

"Sheffield has more clubs and nightspots per head of population than any other city in England, including London. Sheffield people have been spoiled rotten for years, and the wheel had to come off some time."

● "Sheffield people have been spoiled rotten for years, and the wheel had to come off sometime."
Martin Baird

Looking towards the Fiesta and Bonapartes Casino

DiRTY STOP OUT'S GUIDE to 1980s SHEFFIELD

● **"These days, with acute unemployment and no job security, there are just too many clubs in Sheffield."**
Max Omare

Max Omare

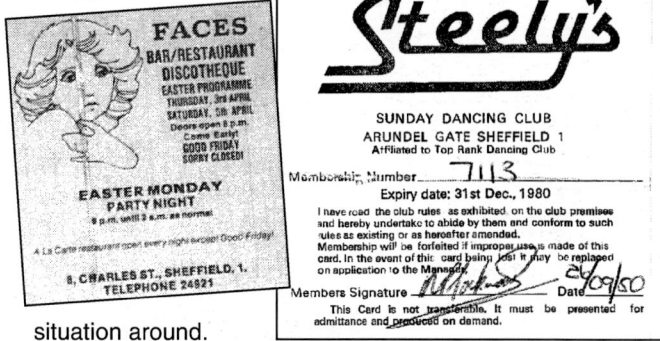

Afterdark impresario Max Omare, who first made his name with Shades on Ecclesall Road a few years earlier, was also suffering.

"I've seen businessmen who used to drink champagne by the magnum, and gallons of gin and tonic now ordering a half of lager", he was reported as saying at the time.

Max, who now had a stable containing Maximillion's, the Mona Lisa and Max's Downtown Cocktail Bar, said:

"The problem is the recession. People haven't got enough spending power so they're far more careful with their money.

"These days, with acute unemployment and no job security, there are just too many clubs in Sheffield."

Max Omare had seen the writing on the wall two years earlier and reined in the amount of nights his Mona Lisa on Rockingham Street was trading. He'd recently invested £250,000 to turn his former Genevieve in Charter Square into the more opulent Maximillions as a way to turn the situation around.

Months later and he was 'considering selling.'

Robert Bradbury, who had been operating Faces on Charles Street, wasn't in a much better position.

"We went through the halcyon days of 1979-80" he said at the time.

"Most of the big steel redundancies took place in 1980 and they had a ball - everyone was going mad.

"Eat, drink and be merry was the motto - for tomorrow the redundancy pay runs out.

"Sheffield started to die in the early summer of 1981.

"Easter was super, but in May and June things started to drop away.

The dividing lines between pubs and clubs - something that barely now exists at all - were already starting to blur in the 1980s as bar licensing hours were extended to 11pm on Fridays and Saturdays leaving punters less time to drink in nightclubs.

"Our customers were coming in 30 minutes to an hour later than before, and over a year that adds up an awful lot of lost business", said Robert Bradbury.

The arrival of eighties style 'fun pubs' which did their utmost to mirror nightclubs, were another body blow to their after hours counterparts.

The only mainstream club that seemed to be weathering the storm was Barker's Pool's finest, Josephine's.

● **Phil Staniland**

"Dingwalls was a legendary venue that always occupied the gig pages of the New Musical Express and other famous music papers.

"To Sheffield this represented a new outlet to see some legendary names particularly in rock. It was like having the Jools Holland Show on your doorstep!

"I remember seeing Bo Diddley there and a kind of rock supergroup that included Bob Weir from the Grateful Dead, Billy Cobham and various other names. I think they were called Bobby and the Midnites. John Cale even did a solo spot there.

"The venue also encouraged local bands too.

"I seem to remember the Bailey Brothers doing the venue a few times and the band I was in at the time, the Mirror Crack'D, had a residency there for a while.

"During the Dingwalls lifetime myself and the singer of the Mirror CrackD, Rick Baines, used to go down to the venue during the day to sort out the odd bit of business - although I can't remember what that would have been now.

"The venue had the most unlikely manager at the time who didn't seem at all to fit into the Dingwalls ethos at all. He seemed better suited to the world of Batley Variety Club and had never heard of anybody that most people interested in music were.

"He was a really nice bloke called Ted and we used to listen to his stories which were invariably linked to 'Opportunity Knocks' or 'Opp Knocks' as he had abbreviated it to.

"Both myself and Rick spent many an hour in his office lapping up his stories from this bygone era referring to the acts as being 'bloody fantastic!!!!'

"You'd hear him talking to someone on the phone about a particular act and he'd be saying 'E's bloody fantastic - 'E's the next Tarbie!!' and then in the next instance he'd be booking The Damned but not knowing who they were.

"He always used 'Opportunity Knocks' as his talent gauge so to speak.

"I remember one time hearing him on the phone with a particular agent and him turning round to everyone present in the office while covering the receiver saying 'Av got a manager 'ere wanting to book somebody called One the Juggler. They've certainly never been on 'Opp Knocks' cause av never fuckin' 'eard er 'em! What shall a do? Shall I book 'em a what?'

"He always used to tell me and Rick that he put Peters and Lee on the road to fame and fortune saying 'yes it were me that introduced 'em to a man in a bar and 't next thing thi were on Opp Knocks and bloody won it - thi were bloody fantastic!!!'"

DiRTY STOP OUT'S GUIDE to 1980s SHEFFIELD

● BEER AND TARTAN SHIRTS AT THE DINGWALLS!

Tony Beesley:

"By 1982 my days of gig-going in Sheffield were decreasing rapidly.

"The two to three gigs a week of the few years previously had narrowed down to a few each month. The Top Rank had past its hey-day and the very last time I went there was in 1983 to see new goth stars, Bauhaus. I left unimpressed. The mod scene was now far more alive in Rotherham than Sheffield by this time and some great nights were had at the Assembly Rooms and Clifton Hall.

"Mods would travel from all over the region and beyond for these reputable nights.

"Some mod-inclined bands performed there too, but it was the records being spun that most impressed me and would help influence my varied musical tastes throughout the rest of the '80s.

"Over in Sheffield there was the Limit club, but that had had its heyday and although some great bands would still perform there almost right up until its demise, the place was quickly descending into a club night-themed venue.

"Consequently, I never stepped into the place again after 1982. The Leadmill was another story. By late '82 and into '83 it was just getting into its stride and some amazing bands performed there. Another new venue had opened too. The old Bierkeller of my older brother's 1970s drinking adventures had re-opened as an off-shoot of the Dingwalls venue of London.

"Only open for a short period of time, the venue managed to attract some great bands and me and my mates ventured to plenty of them: The Damned, Richard Hell, Hanoi Rocks, London Cowboys and others.

"On one occasion me and Barney Rubble went to see Big Country, the new band formed by ex-Skids guitarist, Stuart Adamson. They had only just released their very first single 'Fields Of Fire' and I was very interested in finding out how they cut it live. I was crazy on the Skids. On the night, me and Barney got there and banged a few pints of cider down the neck, quickly buzzing with the affects.

"We tried chatting lasses up, but seeing as we couldn't afford to buy any a drink, we didn't get very far; besides, Barney was now a hitched man and going proper steady, not that it would have deterred him really, though.

"When two older lads asked us to watch their pints while they went for a lash, we said 'Ok, no worries-will do'.

"As the fellas, themselves a bit worse for wear, disappeared, me and Barney took one look at each other and picked up a pint each and supped 'em straight down.

"Right at that moment, Big Country came onto the small Dingwalls stage and started to play and we got up and shot straight to the front. Turning around, I saw the two pint-less blokes arrive back at their table and noticing their pints were supped dry, one of them had got a bloke by the scruff of the neck, blaming the innocent soul for nicking his beer.

● *"Only open for a short period of time, the venue managed to attract some great bands."*

"It was dark, we were crafty and the other guy just happened to be in the wrong place at the wrong-time! The sounds of 'In A Big Country' and Stuart Adamson's almost bagpipe-sounding guitar soundtracked the occasion as me and Barney cracked up laughing like a pair of Mutleys of 'Wacky Races' fame. That night we must have nicked half a dozen pints each from people distracted by the music and spectacle of this fresh new sound from the Highlands.

"Big Country were Scottish and wore tartan checked shirts and pretty soon that was the in-thing to wear for a while.

"That night they played note-for-note perfect renditions of what would become their first album later that year. They did play 'Fields Of Fire' and 'In A Big Country' again for their encore after which we were left wanting more. Their set was pretty quick but was just

Tony Beesley in the early 1980s

enough to whet my appetite for more of their songs.

"Thankfully, I did see Big Country again within the next few weeks, at the very same venue and they were just as amazing to experience - sending out a Celtic vibe of anthemic rock 'n' roll. They soon became a big-selling band with fast selling albums and sell out tours and, along with U2 and Simple Minds, heralded a new era in stadium rock, playing large City Halls.

"I much preferred the experience of seeing them perform in that small and intimate smoke-filled-dimly-lit Dingwalls venue where, for a very short period, their music crossed genres and style and the beer was free!

"Years later, the very talented Stuart Adamson took his own life and there is never a play of a Skids or Big Country record that I hear when I don't mourn his sad passing and often recall those nights at the Sheffield Dingwalls!"
(Extracts taken from Tony Beesley's forthcoming book 'What about the 80's?!' the follow up to 'Kid on a Red Chopper Bike: a ride through the 1980s.)

DiRTY STOP OUT'S GUIDE to 1980s SHEFFIELD

Attercliffe's Horse & Jockey

Not so much the street of dreams (in the sky) in the 1980s on Park Hill

JOSIE'S - THE CHAMPAGNE KING OF 1980S CLUBBING

J osephine's will always be remembered for having probably the strictest after dark entry policies anywhere in the city.

But arguably its most successful banning was that of the eighties recession - the economic meltdown that seriously damaged many of its contemporaries didn't seem to touch the place.

Whilst most venues would do their utmost to attract the potential business on their doorstep, this venue side-stepped the lot of it.

Not surprising really as the venue was surrounded by three institutions that were the very antithesis of everything Josephine's stood for: the NUM headquarters was 100 yards up the road, just round the back was the West Street dole office and the socialist town hall was but a left turn out the door.

Whilst the rest of Sheffield

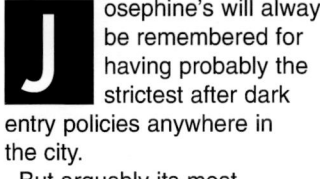

● Josephine's ran a Midas Touch style operation that provided escapism six nights a week

seemed to be enveloped in strikes, Giros and war with central Government, Josephine's ran a Midas Touch-style operation that provided escapism six nights a week.

Maybe it was the smaller capacity and more intimate atmosphere that set it apart; whatever it was, it worked.

Any talk of signing on, feminism or CND was left outside as you were whisked away to a nether world of cocktails, gleaming mirror balls and pulsating disco lights.

The burgeoning feminist movement of the era got short shrift as would-be female bar staff queued up to be kitted out in some of the skimpiest outfits in after dark Sheffield and the venue's 'Miss Lovely Legs' competition attracted all comers.

Sheffield-based entrepreneur Dave Allen was just getting started in the seventies when he unveiled the club.

It was the 1980s when he was the true disco king of Steel City whilst also operating Napoleon's Casino on Ecclesall Road and Bonaparte's Casino in the shadow of the Fiesta cabaret club which crashed and burned for the last time in early 1980 (Bob Bacon, the venue's former manager, ended up being the Josephine's manager).

Whilst most nightclubs played at food or left their punters to chance upon Greasy Vera's (a legendary all-night fast food caravan) and its cheeseburgers on the way home, Dave Allen offered haute cuisine and top class service in the venue's very own restaurant.

Above: Another busy night at Josephine's

All ship shape at The Ship Inn

DiRTY STOP OUT'S GUIDE to 1980s SHEFFIELD

● "I wanted to open a place that people would dress up to come in."

Dave Allen

Josephine's boasted its own champagne league where customers with expensive tastes, who regularly included sports stars, monied-up business people and poseurs galore, could compete for the honour of quaffing the most Dom Perignon in any one month.

"We don't even have to advertise", Dave Allen famously said of the pull of his club in the 1980s.

"I wanted to open a place that people would dress up to come in.

"I think it was well known that if you were going to Josephine's you had to get dressed up as if you were going to a wedding.

"If you wanted to book to get into the restaurant you'd have to book three or four weeks in advance. It was the best restaurant in town bar none."

The venue also pioneered toilet attendants (in both the ladies and gents) armed with every conceivable lotion, potion and perfumery aimed at helping attracting the opposite sex.

Josephine's, which originally opened in 1976, ended up becoming one of Sheffield's longest lasting nightclubs.

It poured its last glass of champagne around the turn of the Millennium.

Its visitor's book became a who's who of sport and entertainment and many punters still haven't got over its demise.

Above: Josephine's staff

LOOK OUT FOR MORE DETAILS IN THE NEXT TWO WEEKS

● Paul Smith

"It was definitely the place to be seen for the jet-set - either aspiring or actual. All the football players would be down there together with the snooker players when the championships were happening in the city."

● Sue Milner

"It was all dodgy looking businessmen leching over the bar staff - fantastic!"

● Trish Sharp

"We'd be there week in and week out, we used to love it there. There was a group of about six of us and when we were skint we used to take it in turns pretending it was one of our hen nights so that we would get free drinks, ahh they were the days!"

DiRTY STOP OUT'S GUIDE to 1980s SHEFFIELD

DiRTY STOP OUT'S GUIDE to 1980s SHEFFIELD

The man with the Midas Touch - Josephine's boss Dave Allen

Josephine's staff

● Paul Smith

"You were never 100% sure the bouncers would let you in. It was a small club, they could afford to be a bit more select.

"We used to say it was the preserve of the unemployed of Dore and Totley who had their own trust funds in the shape of their parents. There were lots of rich old men fawning over blonde bimbo types - we were so jealous!

"If we either failed to get in or failed to pull it was off to Cairo's. If that ended in tears we'd have no choice but to end the night at Roxy's."

DiRTY STOP OUT'S GUIDE to 1980s SHEFFIELD

Josephine's
Barkers Pool
Sheffield 1
Tel. 739810

New Years Eve Extravaganza

Monday 31st December 1984

9 pm through till 2 am

Admission £6

No 045

Gentlemen - We prefer Jackets please

The management reserves the right to refuse admission

Towering doorman Big Jim

DiRTY STOP OUT'S GUIDE to 1980s SHEFFIELD

Josephine's in action

Dave Allen with staff

'ROCK ON THE RATES' WITH THE LEADMILL

CHAPTER THREE

Pelican crossing at the top of Commercial Street with the Marples in the background

Opening early in 1980, The Leadmill added a totally new dimension to Sheffield's night (and day) culture.

Left-leaning protest was its very lifeblood and it stood like an anti-Thatcherite sentinel against a tide of political and economic turmoil.

The Leadmill (or Leadmill Community Arts Co-operative as it was originally known) was the brainchild of a motley crew of students, artists, unemployed and volunteers with a shared vision.

The official line read: "The opening of The Leadmill in 1980 was a response to the lack of cultural facilities in Sheffield and was set against the backdrop of a political and economic environment characterised by the beginning of Thatcherism".

It was billed as 'away from the uptown apocalypse', it definitely was.

The Leadmill originally ran on a succession of 'one-off' licenses to sell alcohol but there was a limit on how long this situation could last.

Their application for a permanent license was refused on the grounds of the building's unsuitability. It ended up closing in September 1980.

But the organisers - including stalwarts like Marcus O'Hagan, Martin Bedford and Phil Mills - put out appeals in the media and their campaign gathered momentum and support.

DiRTY STOP OUT'S GUIDE to 1980s SHEFFIELD

Big Top Theatre, Furnival Road

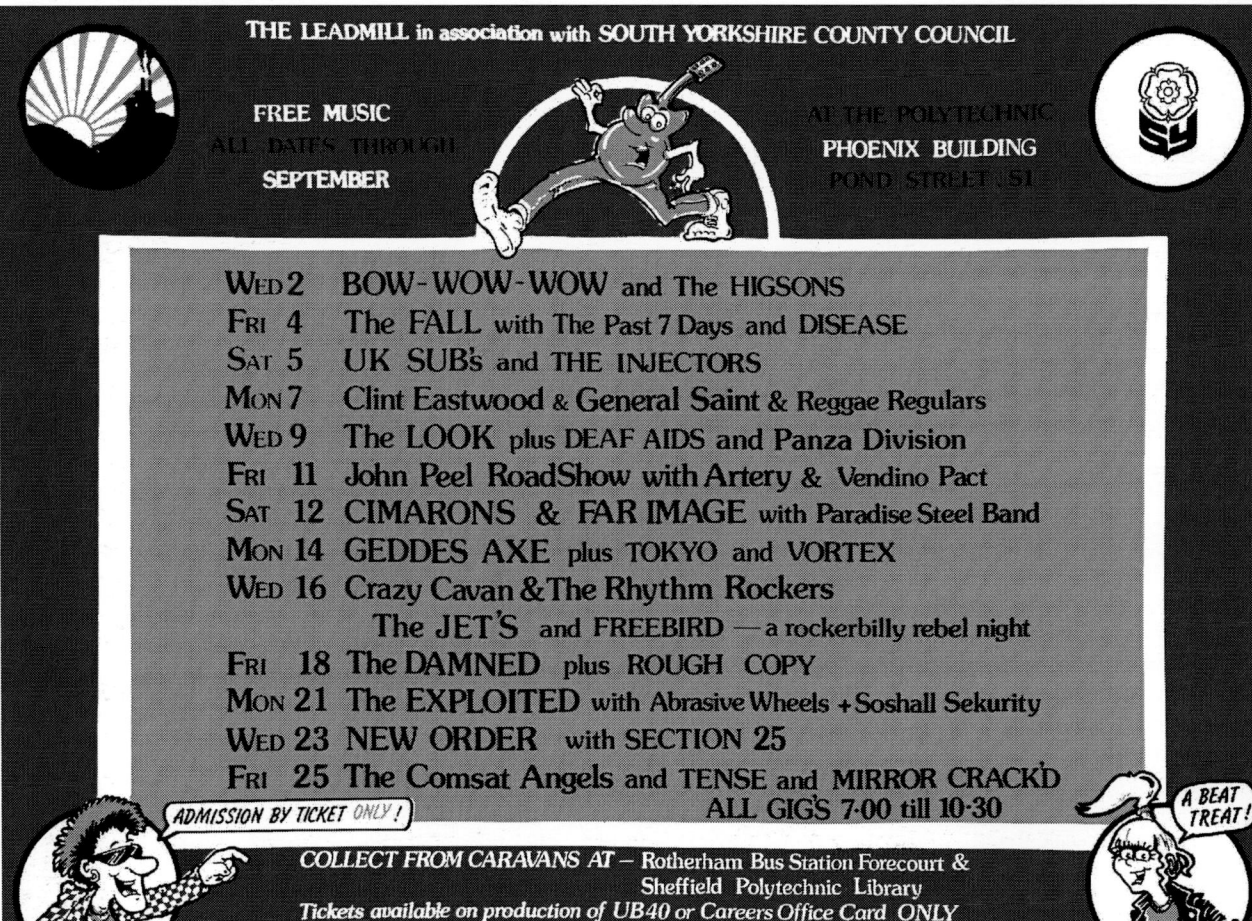

Poster advertising the free gigs for anyone on the dole

Dirty Stop Out's Guide to 1980s Sheffield

The council finally stepped in with a grant of £1,250 to get the ball rolling.

In March 1981 there was a further grant of £22,000 from the Government's Manpower Services Commission in the shape of the Jubilee Fund.

The Leadmill reopened in September 1982 with Prince Charles doing the honours.

In many respects it was going head to head with West Street's Limit which was, up until this point, cleaning up in the live music stakes.

But both venues ended up thriving throughout the era which clearly demonstrates the size of the alternative market in the 1980s.

For many the Leadmill was, at the beginning, the utopian socialist vision in motion.

It became a future cornerstone in an area that would eventually become known as Sheffield's Cultural Industries Quarter and be joined by the nearby Red Tape Studios, the first municipal recording studio in the country, the Site Gallery and The Workstation office space.

It became part of the council's drive to create jobs in non-traditional sectors following the widespread decimation of Sheffield's steel industry that was putting thousands on the dole at the time.

Sheffield City Council, in a visionary move that saw the area become a blueprint for similar ideas right across the world in future years, saw putting their money into culture as an investment for future regeneration.

Left: No self-assuming punk was without a skateboard in 1980s

● **Jane Thomas**

"Whatever happened to Rat Records that seemed to be attached to the front of The Leadmill in the early 1980s?

"Great punk rock record shop with even better carrier bags!

"Did The Leadmill have heating in the early days? It was always absolutely freezing."

● **Paul Barley**

"I think The Clash and its various off-shoots always had a special relationship with Sheffield. The band played their live debut at the Black Swan in 1976 and then guitarist Mick Jones chose The Leadmill for the first live outing of Big Audio Dynamite one Sunday night supporting The Alarm.

"A legendary gig of the era."

DiRTY STOP OUT'S GUIDE to 1980s SHEFFIELD

The first five years or so of The Leadmill were a heady mix of gigs, theatre, workshops, club nights and cheap admission prices.

The names that graced The Leadmill stage in the early years included Pulp, Dead Kennedys, Marc Almond, Big Audio Dynamite, New Order, The Fall, Killing Joke, Cabaret Voltaire, The Pogues and scores of others.

One of their biggest coups was landing Culture Club the week they hit the top spot with 'Do You Really Want To Hurt Me'. Tickets cost 50p...

Leadmill co-ordinator Adrian Vinken said of their stance on prices:

"One has to consider that for a growing proportion of people in the city the only income they've got is unemployment benefit, and the entertainment they can afford isn't going to be £3 and £4 entrance fees and a pound for a pint of lager."

DiRTY STOP OUT'S GUIDE to 1980s SHEFFIELD

● **Andy Stevens**

"I remember seeing the Dead Kennedys there in the early 1982 - it was definitely one of the high-points of my life. I was only about 14. We got there early and were chatting to singer Jello Biafra at their sound check. He seemed a really calm bloke. The same can't be said for a couple of hours later when he was screaming like a man possessed and spending the entire gig crowd surfing.

"I managed to miss school the following morning but it was worth it. All that and the club wasn't even serving alcohol that night. Madness!"

Jarvis Cocker wrote and directed The Leadmill's Christmas panto for kids. It starred 50 musicians from local bands.

He said at the time: "We wanted to see 1982 out in style and make a lot of cool people from pop groups look stupid. I think it's a first for the Steel City, and it's going to be a lot of fun."

Madonna didn't do it for The Leadmill, they turned down her offer the following year (it's fair to say they lived to regret it). She ended up making her UK debut at The Hacienda.

But they had a big hit on their hands with their 'Beat Club' night that started the same the year and saw Peter Stringfellow in regular attendance.

Hull's Housemartins opted to queue to get in their own gig 'because it seemed more democratic'. The bouncers didn't see it that way and refused them entry. The error was later rectified.

By the end of the era there was less art, less politics and a whole lot more commercial rock'n'roll.

The Leadmill had become one of the most successful venues of its type in the country.

Club nights were packed, gigs were packed.

The venue became an acid house pioneer with the launch of 'The Steamer' with resident DJ Graeme Park in 1988. The Leadmill also started trading nights with Manchester's Hacienda and staged early gigs by the Happy Mondays who were then supporting The Shamen.

Live music awards followed and landmark gigs of the late eighties also included Jane's Addiction, Faith No More, Primal Scream and Jesus Jones.

● **DON'T RIOT - WATCH THE DAMNED FREE INSTEAD**

Funding for a series of free concerts was vilified by the national press as a waste of taxpayers' money.

Anyone on the dole in Sheffield in the summer of 1981 had a ball. For thirteen nights at Sheffield Poly you could se anyone from The Damned to New Order at the 'Rock On The Rates' festival.

It was seen as a way to help stop the inner city riots breaking out in Sheffield.

The disturbances that caused millions of pounds in damages to nearby Birmingham and Nottingham never happened here.

Nigel Lockwood drinking at the Leadmill with (left) Sylvia and Rita Fletcher in 1984

Sheffield's best kept secret, The Bath Hotel

THE DECADE OF PROTEST

Sheffield Trades Council march in support of the Miners Strike

When you compare the Blair years to the Thatcherite era it was like living in a different world.

Thatcher became a hate figure largely unparallelled in UK Government whilst the youth growing up in the era of New Labour, until Iraq at least, had forgotten how to protest.

The arguments of the Thatcherite era were rarely confined to Parliament. They permeated society like never before.

Great swathes of the youth of Sheffield and the region did little more than protest for much of the 1980s.

Whilst the Thatcherite era signalled rampant consumerism and wealth creation for some, for the north it meant living under the shadow of the Miner's Strike, the poor getting poorer and gaping class divisions like never before.

Many fell through the cracks altogether. Once Britain had prided itself on not seeing people sleeping on the streets or begging. Not anymore.

Thatcher's policies were viewed by many as manipulative and regularly verging on reckless.

In many respects she was extremely

"So as you raise a glass to the eighties tomorrow night, drink with me to the awakening of Britain.

"If it is to be a dynamic decade for us all, these will be difficult and dangerous years. But we are drinking to a country with a future."

Margaret Thatcher, New Year's message, 1979

lucky. Labour had imploded in the late 1970s when she first came to power and if hadn't have been for Argentina's nationalistic gamble with the Falklands, her government would have probably been destroyed after a single term and 'Thatcherism' would have ended up a half-forgotten joke rather than the malevolent sledgehammer it felt like, for many, at the time.

If it hadn't been for her Falklands victory and feeling of infallibility buoyed up by the media as she swept in on a landslide victory and a second term she might never had taken on the miners.

Great sections of the youth completely fell off the radar in the 1980s. Signing on became a way of life, the black economy mushroomed and life seemed to lurch from inner city riots to Greenham Common protests to the Wapping dispute.

All seemed so rosy for Sheffield as the city's own Seb Coe triumphed at the 1980 Moscow Olympics but it didn't last.

Even the launch of Clive Sinclair's C5 and Roland Rat couldn't save us from the eternal damnation that was life at the bottom of the pile in Thatcher's Britain.

Instead half the youth population turned vegetarian (or vegan if we were being really brave), started squatting (remember the anarchist centre that set up shop near Sheffield Cathedral?) and flew the flag for women's rights.

DiRTY STOP OUT'S GUIDE to 1980s SHEFFIELD

● Ainsley Stones

"The late '80s were when I started to gig in earnest with my bands Bad Taste (their debut single is now worth about £30 a throw in rare vinyl guides - some people will buy any old tat); Epitaph, and by 1989 Bedlam Choir: they were very nearly famous!

"The great thing for me was that I was able to play an awful lot of places that I was nowhere near old enough to drink in, in front of enthusiastic adult audiences.

"I went from being a quiet lad to a rock monster in a matter of months.

"I also learned a lot about what is expected of serious musicians, which stood me in very good stead, as I now do it full time.

"One of my favourite places to play was Take Two, a great venue in Attercliffe, which wasn't nearly as small as some would have you believe and used to attract some significant bands.

"I used to play there every few weeks, initially with Bad Taste, and was given invaluable advice by the owner Marcus Reynolds, a very opinionated but constructive guy. I recall doing a gig there supporting The Farm (who were not nice) and also going to see Doctor Feelgood. That was a busy night! The venue also seemed to have an uncanny liking for death metal bands such as Candlemass and psychobilly bands too, like the Radiacs. Great times.

"Other notable "lost" venues included The Locarno on London Road, which I played at in both Bad Taste and

Bedlam Choir

Bedlam Choir (supporting Lawnmower Deth), The Penguin at Shiregreen, The Owl in Neepsend (where we managed to offend a visiting biker gang), Marples (where my grandad, some 77 years old, came to watch us and said "much better than all the dance music rubbish in the charts!"), George IV on Infirmary Road (I later found out my mum was a go-go dancer there in the early '70s!), and of course the legendary Hallamshire Hotel on West Street."

DiRTY STOP OUT'S GUIDE to 1980s SHEFFIELD

Food parcels for miners at Beighton Miners Welfare Club

Sheffield Women Against Pit Closures trip to London

DiRTY STOP OUT'S GUIDE to 1980s SHEFFIELD

Left: Even playing guitar became an issue for the police in the era

Below: Sheffield Women Against Clause 28 Day of Action

The Anvil in Charter Square

Tories hammer Anvil

Brick trams on The Moor - they probably looked good on paper...

REBELS, ROCKERS AND TOTAL 'HYSTERIA'

Above left: Life at The Wapentake

Whilst Sheffield's steel industry was left in disarray in the early 1980s, another very different strain of metal was set to become one of the city's most successful world-wide exports of the era.

The career of Def Leppard went stratospheric as the band took on the USA and won, often to the horror of their local fans who thought they'd been dropped in favour of the bright lights of LA.

It was an era of unbelievable highs (their 'Hysteria' album sold over 15 million copies) and heart-rendering lows (drummer Rick Allen lost his arm after crashing his new Chevrolet Corvette Stingray on the A57 near Sheffield on New Year's Eve, 1984) for the band who are as still as big today as they ever were.

It's fair to say that Sheffield had more than a little influence on the shape of the metal scene that took the country and much of the world by storm in eighties as it spawned acts, venues and personalities that defined the genre at its most prolific (and regularly, many would argue, most ridiculous).

Things could have gone either way for South Yorkshire's finest, Saxon, with Sheffield's own Pete Gill on drums.

Their ferocious sonic metal assault actually got the green light from many a punk when they were playing early support slots with the likes of The Clash.

But they became a forerunner of the New Wave of British Heavy Metal movement alongside the rejuvenated Iron Maiden fronted by local boy, Bruce Dickenson.

Rebels was, without a doubt, Sheffield's rock club, numero uno.

The Dixon Lane operation flew the metal flag for the entire era.

Joseph Wild:
"I'd regularly go there four nights a week. It was awesome and the women were amazing!"

The venue was originally opened by Peter Stringfellow as The Penthouse in the late 1960s. Almost as legendary as the venue, in a bizarre sort of way, was the journey to the hallowed doors themselves, via seven flights of stairs.

Rebels was the brainchild of former Limit club bouncer Steve Baxendale. He was already a biker and the opening his own club seemed the next logical step.

DiRTY STOP OUT'S GUIDE to 1980s SHEFFIELD

Rebels in action

DiRTY STOP OUT'S GUIDE to 1980s SHEFFIELD

Bob Maltby was the original Rebels DJ. He was later succeeded by Lez Wright.

He said: "We had some great times. The coming and going of different age groups and different types of music was interesting. Different eras like glam rock and your AOR stuff.

"Mid '80s was really good for the women. The dance floor was just packed out with them."

Everyone from Griff Rhys Jones (a rock fan on the sly) to Peter Stringfellow frequented the place, the latter checking out what his former venue was looking like after a rock injection.

Chris Twiby:
"Who could forget the friendly atmosphere as if we were all one big rock community? A club that really stuck to its metal values. I fell down the stairs a few times too. Joined in the piano sing-a-long at the old timers pub at the bottom of the road and got my clothes from Pippy's on Cambridge Street. Great days."

There was also the nearby Yorkshireman, Sportsman and other hard drinking, hard rocking establishments.

But on the pub front nowhere really came close to Olga Marshall's Wapentake.

The sprawling cellar bar reigned supreme through the decade. Rockers, punks, bikers - it was a melting pot for anyone seeking to avoid frequenting nearby townie venues like Cairos, Isabella's and others.

Newcastle Brown was consumed by the lorry load, the music was of a volume to shake the building's very foundations and, despite its hard exterior, it enjoyed a largely trouble-free existence.

Its reputation, and that of the burgeoning Sheffield rock scene as a whole, even came to the attention of The Guardian as far back as 1980.

They did a massive spread on the place.

Reporter Mary Harron said: "The Wapentake is a modern pub in the centre of Sheffield, as anonymous as any other, but in the evenings it is like a secret clubhouse. The regulars are nearly all in their late teens or early twenties, and they come for one reason: to hear the heavy metal records that the resident DJ plays all night at ear-shattering volume.

"Subtlety has no place in heavy metal. Critics have called it the worst form of rock music ever invented, but no form of rock music ever invented inspires such passionately devoted fans; the success of heavy metal is the phenomenon of the year in British rock."

Above: Wapentake matriarch Olga Marshall

Inset: Wapentake DJ Ken Hall

Above: Life at the Wapentake   Below: Sheffield Rockers

REBELS
NO 1 ROCK CLUB

ROCK 9.00 p.m. to 2.00 a.m.   20–22 Dixon Lane, Sheffield 0742 755060

MONDAY 2nd & 4th Week of the Month
Alternative ROCK MUSIC
FREE ADMISSION

WEDNESDAY
ROCK – HARD ROCK – AOR MUSIC
50p Admission
£1 Drinks

THURSDAY
ROCK – HARD ROCK – AOR MUSIC
50p Admission
£1 Drinks

FRIDAY
ROCK – HARD ROCK – AOR MUSIC
£2.50 (before 11.30 p.m.)
£4.00 (after)

SATURDAY
AMERICAN ROCK
£2.50 (before 11.30 p.m.)
£4.00 (after)

REBELS ROCK DJ'S

LES (The Rebel)..............

VIKING MARK......

PADDY...................
(From the Derby Rock House)

MARK DALE............

ANDY COPPING.....
From The Nottingham Rock City
Top Quality CD Sound

THE BAILEY BROS
An Audio Visual Rock Experience

The Magnificent Seven

Ring 755060
for details

DiRTY STOP OUT'S GUIDE to 1980s SHEFFIELD

Below: Roxy's Miss Glam Rock Competition

The cranking of the glam scene up to eleven and beyond actually came from a rather unlikely source - Barry Noble's sprawling Roxy in the former Top Rank building on Arundel Gate.

Their Roxy's Rock Night was a total phenomenon at its height and must have been a financial and trouble-free dream come true for the venue.

Its black and silver 'The Roxy Heavy Rock' membership cards became true badges of honour for the glam kids from across the region.

Sheffield could probably have sustained a far bigger weekend rock club than Rebels; Roxy proved that, but the rockers were quite happy to have a change of scenery on Arundel Gate every other Monday and enjoy their more intimate Rebels home on a Friday and Saturday.

The Roxy night, which started in 1987, was rammed to near capacity at its height - not bad considering it was held on a school night.

The event became one of the most popular bouncer shifts because the women were generally stunning and the only hint of trouble was the odd hissy fit in the gents.

People would regularly travel from right across the country to the event and its Miss Glam Rock Competition became the stuff of legend.

Nearby pubs like Mulberry Tavern and The Yorkshireman were packed to capacity and the night was a far cry from the warzone that was the venue's normal weekend offering.

Graham Wild of Roxy said:

"It was the Roxy management at the time that decided on a rock night. It was a couple of students that worked there at the time and were into rock themselves that suggested it and it took off from there.

"The management at the time were Mike Powell, general manager, and Kevan Dobson, deputy manager.

"They saw what was happening at the top of Dixon Lane and seized the opportunity to capitalise on the rock scene, this in turn increased the Monday night and in turn Wednesday nights popularity and vastly increased the people that turned up to Roxy's."

● SHAUN STEVENSON ON ROXY ROCK NIGHT

"Steve, Eric and I used to go in full stage gear and I remember one night we fell out over something and Steve threw his pint at Eric.

"Eric then went to the bar stormed off and appeared a few minutes later on the stairs above and behind us. We only spotted him when he poured a full pint over Steve.

"Dripping wet they chased each other around the place until they were too knackered to fight and ended up wrestling on the floor.

"When the bouncers turned up I sent them packing by telling them that we were having "creative differences".

"I also remember tripping over the last step going upstairs, completely falling over and managing to retain every drop of the vodka and orange I was carrying

"I recall dancing like a loon most times - my personal favourite was the laying on the floor and running around in circles on the spot.

"I never took part in this but I distinctly remember Fish Dancing - the basic principle was to lay on the floor and flap around like a fish out of water.

This did provide a terrific spectacle if you had a number of people doing it but on your own I suspect people were worried about some kind of epileptic fit."

● CAROLINE GOWING REMEMBERS THE ROCK NIGHT AT ROXY

"It's hard to imagine now that the biggest night out of the month would be on a Monday, but we looked forward to the Roxy's Rock Night with great anticipation. It was so exciting to get out to a proper club and despite having no jobs and no cash we'd be on a mission to get there.

"Everyone would be asking each other if they were going in the weeks leading up to it and you just had to make it for the experience. It was so popular, one of the local rockers even hired a bus and sold tickets for it.

"I got there in a car full of lads and lasses - rock rebels with attitude, taken by a good friend with a very reliable mum, who'd drive us there and drop us on the doorstep and get us home safely afterwards!

"It was a big car and it was naturally packed on the way there and if it wasn't, it seemed to be filled on the way back with the odd extra stowaway if there was any room left.

"The Roxy seemed huge to us - our rock nights in Chesterfield were held at the tiny Adam and Eve nightclub, with the same folks week in week out.

"It was like a celebration going somewhere with hundreds of new faces, with bigger hair and some spectacular dress sense. There were old and young rockers united and the incredibly loud and hair-raising music appealed to everyone, airing classic tracks and the latest new hits from the rock charts, which were all floor fillers.

"Our Chesterfield blokes scrubbed up well for the occasion - you had to make the effort in Sheffield. The spree to the Roxy was our event of the month.

"A typical night for our gang would start off with the lads heading for the downstairs bar at the back and me and my friend heading upstairs to the balcony for a good people watching position. The place would be heaving and head banging. There'd be some competitive displays of fashion and makeup in the glam rock horde, we'd have fun trying to guess which were the men and which were the women.

"We'd have a few patrols around the club during the evening to see who and what we could spot. Then we'd hit the dance floor, stick to it, skid on it, get lost in the dry ice and surf along to Dave Lee Roth's version of the Beach Boys' 'California Girls', sliding around with air guitars at the ready for Whitesnake's 'Still of the Night'.

"We'd always end up back with the lads we'd arrived with by the early hours, our trusty lift faithfully waiting for us at 2.30am. We'd all be messing around on the steps outside not wanting to leave. My friend's mum was so patient with us. On the way home we'd be outrageously misbehaving on the back seat, someone would usually want to stop for a leak on the lay-by of the dual carriageway; there'd be lots of drunken banter and daft jokes, and singing along to Skid Row's '18 and Life'. Unforgettable happiness - I'd love to do it all again, even on a Monday!"

Roxy's Miss Glam Rock Competition

● Jane Lett

"Those stairs at Rebels used to go on, and on, and on. I think there were seven flights of them. I never fell down them but I knew a few people, obviously the worse for drink, who did. I did try the burger van a few times that always sat at the top of Dixon Lane at closing time. Don't think the food was that bad but I probably didn't really care at 2.30am..."

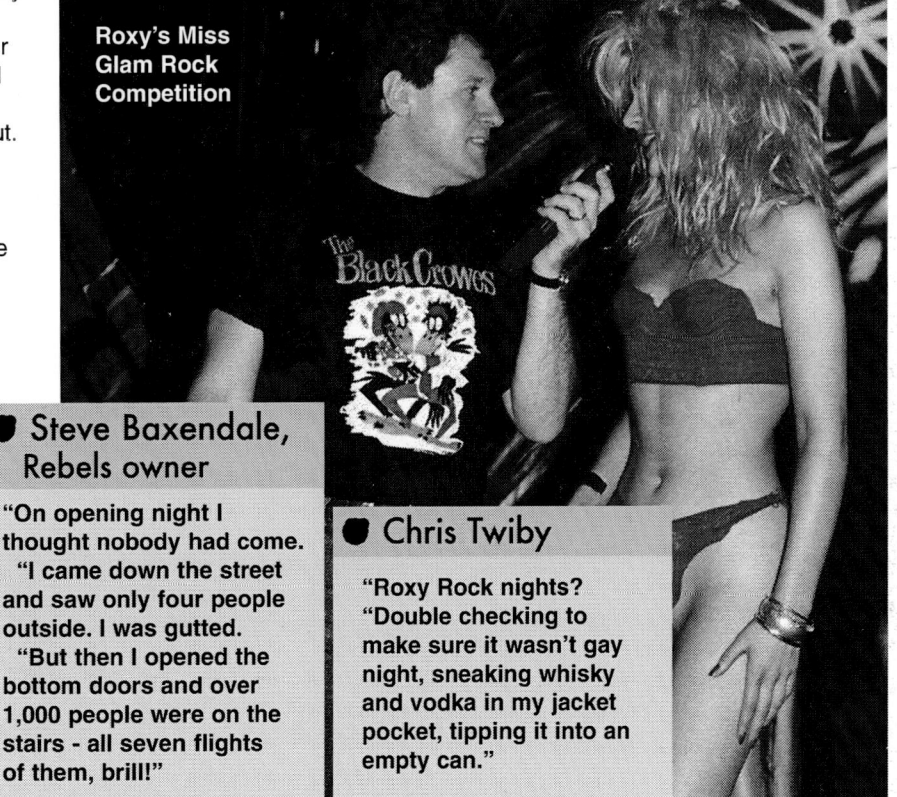

● Steve Baxendale, Rebels owner

"On opening night I thought nobody had come.

"I came down the street and saw only four people outside. I was gutted.

"But then I opened the bottom doors and over 1,000 people were on the stairs - all seven flights of them, brill!"

● Chris Twiby

"Roxy Rock nights?
"Double checking to make sure it wasn't gay night, sneaking whisky and vodka in my jacket pocket, tipping it into an empty can."

DiRTY STOP OUT'S GUIDE to 1980s SHEFFIELD

● SHEFFIELD'S OWN MTV STARS

MTV stars Mick and Dez Bailey

The Bailey Brothers and Mr Big

Probably the most jaw dropping metal career of the decade has to go to the Bailey Brothers. They ended up as two of the most influential voices on the planet as they criss crossed Europe and the globe fronting MTV's first heavy metal show.

How they got there is the stuff of fairytales but was also well deserved.

The two former miners were already veterans of the heavy metal DJ circuit by 1980 having made their debut at Killamarsh Village Centre three years earlier and were slowly rising through the ranks via a Retford Porterhouse residency and having their charts listed in music weekly, Sounds. But it was their surprise appearance on the front cover of Time Out in 1980 with the headline 'WHY ARE THESE MEN PLAYING CARDBOARD GUITARS?' that was the tipping point of their career.

Their DJ road show headlined the UK with a countrywide tour; they boasted residencies everywhere and then, when they thought their career couldn't get any better, they were asked to present the first rock show on the then fledgling MTV.

It became the number one rated show on the channel and the management were totally baffled as to why!

"They ended up calling a specific board meeting one week to try and fathom out why we were so popular," Dez Bailey said. They became the hosts of Donington's Monsters of Rock, interviewed virtually every metal star of the era and were regularly seen as pioneers of the 'air guitar'.

Mick and Dez Bailey today

'IS THAT ALRIGHT FOR YOUSE?' ENTER THE ROXY

If the chance to mix with the glitterati set of Josephine's didn't grab you there were party opportunities a plenty at two of the city centre's brasher, more cavernous counterparts.

The air-craft hanger-style Roxy, sited on Arundel Gate, together with the sprawling Cairo Jax (which started the era as Romeo and Juliet's) on Bank Street were both shamelessly mass market and boasted punters that seemed to buy their entire wardrobe at Burton's or Chelsea Girl.

They were clubbing-style cattle markets on an industrial scale and, despite much of the more 'high-brow' night scene looking down their noses at them, they had as loyal a following as anyone (a 2010 Roxy reunion was a 2,500 sell-out).

The Roxy first appeared in the former Top Rank building in the mid 1980s. It was opened by Barry Noble, a Geordie who advertised the venue on TV with the catchphrase 'is that all right for youse?'

It was definitely all right for Sheffield but Barry, arguably less so - he was reported as dying from a heart attack eight months later.

The Roxy played host to massive stars of the day including Kylie Minogue and Jason Donovan in a world then besotted by Aussie soap, 'Neighbours'.

But it was record producer Pete Waterman bringing his live version of 'The Hitman and Her' TV show that took gave the Roxy a profile like no other in the region.

Along with sidekick, presenter Michaela Strachan, they somehow turned a drunken, unsightly nightclub audience into addictive viewing complete with regular party games and dance spots.

On paper it looks like a total dog's dinner of a formula but, considering most of their target audience would have already consumed copious amounts of lager when it was screened in the early hours of Sunday morning it somehow managed to amass a large cult following and was on air for nearly four years.

The Roxy tried, and mostly succeeded, with every permutation of club night going. 'Grab A Granny' on a Thursday, gay night, rock night and student night to name but a few.

The 2,500 capacity venue was regularly attracting 7,000 party-goers every week.

Weekend fights went with the territory and the venue soldiered on well into the mid 1990s.

Cairo Jax was rather a different set up but with a quite a similar audience. The Bank Street building started life in the 1960s as The Cavendish cabaret club.

It then became Baileys before reopening as Romeo & Juliet's and then Cairo Jax in the 1980s and 1990s.

Half the size of Roxy, it still boasted six bars, diner and lots more.

BARRY NOBLE'S ROXY
Wednesday 50p NIGHT
Beer, Lager, Cider and Spirits
ALL 50P
The Best 'Pintsworth' in town
ROXY OPEN
Wednesday, Thursday, Friday and Saturday
8 pm - 2 am
"Is that alright Fyuzs"

... EVERY MONDAY A SUMMER GROOVE
We're having a Tropical HEATWAVE

Penny's Nightscene

open 9pm to 2am
EYRE STREET
SHEFFIELD
Tel. 28403

FREE ADMISSION
ADMIT ONE on presentation of this ticket at the paydesk. The Management reserve the right to refuse admission. Minimum age 18.

CHAPTER FIVE

CAFE BAR CULTURE ARRIVES ON CAMBRIDGE STREET

Peter McNerney:
"You know, that place that use to be a posh car showroom'.

"That's how I first heard about Henry's on Cambridge Street in the city centre, or more aptly for Sheffield folk, in "Town".

"Having passed the age for drinking legally back in the late seventies, nights out were either pubs or clubs, or for the best nights out, both.

"Then in the early eighties along came Henry's. Not a pub or club but a "cafe bar". It offered the bizarre notion that you could be having a coffee while your mate was having a pint.

"What's the point in that! But that funny foreign stuff was reserved for the day.

"At night the beautiful people of Sheffield would put on their evening finery and head to Henry's for a cocktail with the requisite little umbrella or a selection of "continental" lagers. I recall large G and Ts were popular. And all this under the watchful gaze of no bouncers, sorry doorstaff as we must now call them.

● **Russ Smith**

"I Used to get tanked in Silks and fall into Cairos next door. One side had dance music as it was just as acid house was kicking in and the other side had all the party crap. There was always someone to get off with in the corridors. Brilliant place. Always preferred it to Roxy as that always seemed to be full of 16 year olds trying to get off with housewives whilst Josephine's was all plastic poseurs."

"Compare that with a trip into town on a Friday night now. You'd be forgiven for thinking you'd wandered into central Beirut.*

"It was rowdy of course, but you could hear yourself speak and although it wasn't Club Tropicana (where drinks were apparenlty free) everyone had a great value night out.

"Now time to pack away the rose tinted spectacles . That's because they would have been in danger of being crushed as you fell to the floor at Henry's after being trapped by the crowds against Britain's most 'inappropriate' fountain. It no doubt looked good on the plans and in the day was a nice feature, located just inside the main entrance on the ground floor. There was an upstairs but that might as well have been in Rotherham because no one ventured there.

"The fountain was big enough to stop the traffic on the M1 and some nights you had to climb over it to get back to your table. We may have been young, but we still liked a table.

"And then, one day, it was gone. The whole area opened out and more accessible. It could have been an early victim of the notorious "Elf 'n' Safety". But since we're talking

Peter McNerney

'Ashes to Ashes' years, I'm guessing it was a way of enticing more heavily shoulder padded lovelies to sip on their Brandy Alexanders.

"Closing time was still earlier than when most of today's young people venture out, but by 11pm it was home-time courtesy of a chum who was the perfect person to hang out with at Henry's. He only drank Diet Coke and he had a posh car.

"I shall always remember the crest-fallen look on the traffic officers who would regularly pull over a Ford Escort Cabriolet full of merry twenty-somethings only to discover the driver was a teetotal junior barrister."

*Back in the early 1980's war-torn Beirut was used to describe devastated and dangerous areas.

Looking down Cambridge Street

DIRTY STOP OUT'S GUIDE to 1980s SHEFFIELD

45

GRANELLI'S

Granelli's in Sheaf Market

● Jill Smith

"Always better known as the 'Poxy Roxy'! I first went when I was about 15 - they seemed to let anyone in and some of the sights in there were unbelievable! I was truly shocked. I had a great first night but there was a pitched battle going on at the bottom of the ramp on the way out that was a bit scary.

"I met my ex-fiance there in around 1986. I was 15 and he was 16 - we didn't last! Class! I ended up spending most of my youth in there, it was great.

"We used to go upstairs and look over the balcony to see if we could see any nice men on the dance floor.

"There were so many different things to do. Two dance floors, the amazing lightshow, snogging on the stairs and getting in everyone's way, and so many different bars."

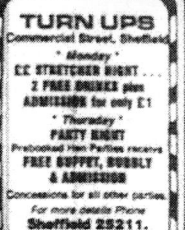

● Rachel Mellor

"I asked my friend what she remembered about the night at Cairo Jax. She couldn't remember the evening. Or Cairo Jax. Or much of the '80s for that matter. But I remember you Cairo Jax.

"The night is embedded in my mind forever like your childhood pet being run over in front of you.

"It truly was the inner circle of Dante's Inferno. It was ridiculously hot, presumably to encourage the punters to bare their grisly bodies as they gyrated. The clientele were raw white trash, all poor teeth and stringy hair.

"I felt unclean just being there. The music was the worst bit though. '80s pop, merging into the aural equivalent of having your skin removed and being rolled in salt. Let's just say I didn't have a very nice time. At all."

Romeo's & Juliet's — THE ONLY PLACE TO BE AROUND CHRISTMAS — we're open for dancing all over the festive period including CHRISTMAS EVE, BOXING DAY, NEW YEAR'S EVE. There's non-stop music with top DJ's and live bands. There's a choice of bars. All in luxurious surroundings. So make more of your party at RJ's this Christmas.
BANK STREET, SHEFFIELD S1 2DR. TEL: 0742 2951

CELEBRATE AT Raffles
RESTAURANT & DISCOTHEQUE
8, CHARLES ST., SHEFFIELD, 1.
FOR RESERVATIONS TELEPHONE
24921 or 754662.

TURN UPS
Commercial Street, Sheffield
* Monday *
££ STRETCHER NIGHT
2 FREE DRINKS plus
ADMISSION for only £1
* Thursday *
PARTY NIGHT
Prebooked Hen Parties receive
FREE SUPPER, BUBBLY
& ADMISSION
Concessions for all other parties.
For more details Phone
Sheffield 25211.

STEELYS PRESENTS DISCO DANCER
CARLING Black Label LAGER
The Disco Dancer Contest
SPONSORED BY CARLING BLACK LABEL LAGER
£100 CASH PRIZE MUST BE WON IN OUR AREA FINAL
£1000 IN CASH PRIZES TO BE WON IN THE NATIONAL FINAL
AREA HEATS: SATURDAY, APRIL 26th.
GET YOUR ENTRY FORM NOW!

DiRTY STOP OUT'S GUIDE to 1980s SHEFFIELD

The Gaumont in Barker's Pool

A Parson Cross night out

Getting married in the 1980s

● **Rita Collins**

"Dancing round our handbags on a weekend.

"Fantastic. What a place!

"If all else failed you could be sure of pulling at the Roxy! We regularly used to do Cairo Jax on Friday and then The Roxy on Saturday and then the late night bus home."

● **Hazel Knight**

"I had my 18th birthday party in Cairos. I think we started at the Underground, then Stonehouse and then Silks next door. It was all going well until the zip on my skin tight dress snapped revealing everything! I thought my night was in tatters until my friend came back with a needle and cotton she'd borrowed off the kind lady in the toilets. Twenty minutes later and I was back on the dance floor. Happy days!"

DiRTY STOP OUT'S GUIDE to 1980s SHEFFIELD

47

Steely's
ARUNDEL GATE. SHEFFIELD I.
9 till 12
Resident DJ STEVE VAUGHAN
See our new lighting direct from America.
TEL. 21927/8

Sheaf Valley Baths - a good Sunday hangover cure

Mary Givens (right) and friend on night out

Nalgo Nursery Nurses and Child Care Assistants protest outside Sheffield Town Hall

Support Child Care Assistants

Fair pay for Nursery Nurses

DiRTY STOP OUT'S GUIDE to 1980s SHEFFIELD

Bill with greyhound and lurcher on Parson Cross

Judy's ladies hairdressing salon, Buchanan Road, Parson Cross

● Paul Smith

"It was all Rick Astley, Luther Vandross and drunken 18 year olds doing 'Oops Upside Your Head' sat on the floor at Cairos.

"There was Silks bar next door as well.

"Definitely a big part of my youth all the same."

David's Place (formerly the Ritz Cinema), Southey Green

DIRTY STOP OUT'S GUIDE to 1980s SHEFFIELD

49

Party goers in Legends

Sharrow Lane lollipop ladies

The Town Hall's 'eggbox' extension and the 'wedding cake' register office next door

DiRTY STOP OUT'S GUIDE to 1980s SHEFFIELD

DiRTY STOP OUT'S GUIDE to 1980s SHEFFIELD

ROCK N ROLL IS ALIVE AND WELL...
AND LIVING ON STANIFORTH ROAD

Attercliffe's Take Two club was definitely an enigma. Where did it come from, where did it go and was it really there at all? It came at a time when new music had all but stopped...

Punk was dead, Indie hadn't done much since The Smiths and the only music filling the arenas seemed to be glam-charged metal.

In terms of a business model, Staniforth Road's Take Two seemed, at best, questionable. But, to the surprise of many, it worked and cool people, it

● **In terms of a business model, Staniforth Road's Take Two seemed, at best, questionable.**

seemed, were quite happy to travel out to darkest Attercliffe for a night out.

It took a bus ride to get there, there seemed to be no decent pubs within a four mile radius and no one seems to have any idea how they got home again but Take Two, for a few years, kept the wolves from the doors and proved you didn't need to be on West Street or Leadmill Road to keep the left of centre generation in wine (or lager), women (and men), and song.

**Left:
The Alarm take a break from rehearsing at Attercliffe's Take Two**

CHAPTER SIX

DiRTY STOP OUT'S GUIDE to 1980s SHEFFIELD

● FORMER MUSIC WRITER OF THE STAR JOHN QUINN:

"When Take Two opened circa 1986 people weren't quite sure what to make of it. The brainchild of Marcus Reynolds, it seemed too far out of the way to be a success.

"Attercliffe wasn't exactly known as a hotbed of indie music.

"Marcus was very tolerant of the ranks of punks, psychobillies, skinheads and assorted ne'r-do-wells who frequented the venue, and this policy of politeness paid off.

"I can't recall there ever being trouble at this particular place. There is a tale about the eternally-over-rated Stone Roses making their Sheffield debut and getting into a scuffle before taking to the stage because the support act had placed a Confederate flag there. I don't know the outcome but as the saying goes, it ain't over till the flat laddie sings.

"Of course the out-of-town status may have had something to do with this. There have probably been academic studies done on this but I reckon you're less likely to wreck a venue if you have to make a real effort to get to it, no matter how bad the reputation of any particular youth group. And anyway, most of the city centre trouble was caused by the 'normal' people. There is another saying that you shouldn't piss on your own doorstep. Well, a large proportion of Sheffield's youth seemed to take this to heart and save it all up until Friday and Saturday when they could do it on other people's. That's when they weren't just trying to prove they were big hitters by acting big and hitting people. Believe me, it was a jungle out there.

"For the most part of clubbing in the city centre I was a Limit and Leadmill man. They played decent music, had bands appearing live, were reasonably safe and there was a decent mix of people, unlike the likes of Josephine's, which seemed to be almost entirely populated by besuited middle-aged men trying to cop off with impressionable young women.

"And infuriatingly often succeeding.

"For those who couldn't carry off the alleged sophistication required to get in, there were the likes of Cairo Jax, Barry Noble's Roxy and Turn-Ups (which a friend once described as 'like the Top Of The Pops studio').

"These were always full of (as my mum used to say) young people enjoying themselves, so I would go - forced into it obviously - determined to look down on the mainstream herds dancing to (pah!) chart pop like the peasants they were. They were quite good occasionally, although I wouldn't admit it at the time. Also, miles from civilisation, there was Fannys at Owler Bar, a place that recently came up in a conversation after being forgotten about for years. It turns out that I had a similar experience to my friends in that it was a place everyone tried once. But only once.

The Toy Shop

DiRTY STOP OUT'S GUIDE to 1980s SHEFFIELD

"Back in the city centre(ish) the music at rock bar Rebels wasn't to my taste at all, but it had a decent atmosphere. Actually looking back it had a strange atmosphere but this is probably due to being six thousand feet above sea level, with a couple of stairs for every foot.

"They should really have supplied oxygen (or at the very least a round of applause) to everyone who actually made it into the place. And then there were of course the dance nights like Jive Turkey at Occasions (and occasionally the City Hall Ballroom) and ones I've totally forgotten the name of at Isabella's. However, that's another story. Or should be...

"Many of these nights out blend into one, but there were the occasional ones that stood out. In Neil Anderson's previous tome, 'Take It To The Limit', I described having my first proper kiss in those illustrious surroundings. Well the Leadmill helped me take things a bit further, if you know what I mean, hur hur. A night when I went down on my own and ended up losing my brand new sweater led to a chain of events that resembled a scene from a 'Carry On' film. I can honestly say I had nothing whatsoever to do with it. Even today hearing Sultans Of Ping FC's 'Where's Me Jumper?' (which actually came out a good few years later - I may be tragic but I'm not quite that tragic) brings a lump to my...er...throat. Oh yeah, this took place on a Friday the 13th. It would.

"Quickly changing the subject, in 1987 I became editor of The Star's pop page so I was a regular writer about and visitor to Take Two, mainly a live music venue but also occasionally the place for indie music discos. They say about the sixties that if you can remember it you weren't there. I was definitely there in the late eighties... but still can't remember much of it. Maybe it's just the passage of time or early onset of senile dementia, but for instance a friend reckons that I went to see The Charlatans (who were always better than the Stone Roses by the way) with her when they also made their local debut at Take Two, but I have absolutely no recollection of it. Maybe it was all a dream. Women often dream about me. In my dreams.

"People go on about the power of the press. Maybe on a national level, but local music journalists tend to delude themselves - I know I did - that what they write is somehow important. It may be a bit to the local bands we write about (that Pulp lot would never have made it without me, blah blah blah) but on a general level it doesn't matter one jot.

● *"They should have supplied oxygen (or at the very least a round of applause) to everyone who actually made it to the place."*

"This was proved to me when Take Two played host to a Northern Irish band called Bam Bam And The Calling who I'd described on the pop page as 'better than The Beatles' on the grounds that one of them was actually called Paul McCartney and as a sulky early-20s punk fan I wasn't too fond of the Fab Four at the time. Their first single was produced by song writing god John O'Neill, of Undertones/That Petrol Emotion fame and the latter band were actually named after one of their numbers. How could they possibly fail? This shameless bit of hype led to them attracting a massive audience of...ooh...four.

"Which wasn't fab, but I bravely fought my way to the front and enjoyed them anyway.

"However the venue had some bigger names too. Primal Scream and Dinosaur Jr played to full houses, while the Lee Brilleaux-led late-80s line-up of Dr Feelgood and punk veterans UK Subs seemed to be in a competition to see who could play there most often. Another act which appeared had an actual chart-topper in their line-up. The Gargoyles contained two former members of The Housemartins, including the pre-prison Hugh Whitaker but it was their singer who stole the show by not only taking over the stage but the entire venue, and even performing one number from outside. Fantastic live band who just couldn't carry it off on record.

"As for local bands, there were lots and lots as Marcus was always willing to give unknown acts a chance. I saw loads, many of whom I wouldn't recognise today. Ones that have stuck in the mind include The Radiacs, Muzzle Club and Slopdosh Bobbar and Ivan Crump. I'm back in touch with some of these people today thanks to the joys of Facebook, so I'd just like to say you should have all made it to the top. Is that okay lads?

"The premature closure of the venue left one less outlet for local and left-field acts to peddle their wares. Marcus was last seen in Sheffield busking with his trombone on Fargate then vanished.

"It turns out that he'd been playing in various cabaret acts and on cruise ships and he now has his own Big Band and a website advertising 'stress-free music' which is not a description that could be applied to many acts that played his venue. They may not have been to his personal taste but Marcus made his mark on us by bringing us some superb shows.

"It's a shame there wasn't a second chance for Take Two.

"And I still think Bam Bam And The Calling were better than The Beatles."

Looking mysterious in the 1980s

DiRTY STOP OUT'S GUIDE to 1980s SHEFFIELD

Inside Angel Street's ABC

Raising a glass as the good times return

S. Yorks. cheap fares stay as they are says bus chief

DiRTY STOP OUT'S GUIDE to 1980s SHEFFIELD

Peters and Lee split up

SINGING STARS Peters and Lee are splitting up.

A spokesman for the blind singer and his Sheffield-born partner, Di Lee, said: "It is an amicable parting, they feel that they have done everything and they are now looking forward to the challenge of resuming their own careers."

The split has brought to an end one of the showbiz legends of recent times.

Lennie was a blind pianist-singer who made a good living playing the cabaret clubs.

Di, born Dianne Littlebates in Shirecliffe, was half of the Hailey twins dancing duo with her cousin Liz. They kept meeting on cabaret engagements and when Liz decided to go solo, Di teamed up with Lennie in 1970.

Charts

Their fairy story rise to the top took three years. Their break came on Opportunity Knocks and they played on the show for weeks.

The unique boy and girl singing duo touched the nation's hearts. Their debut single, Welcome Home, topped the charts for weeks in 1973 and they starred in the Royal Variety Performance before the Queen at the London Palladium.

In 1974 they topped the bill at Blackpool's North Pier for a season, registering the biggest triumph the resort had ever seen. They played for eight weeks without a seat unsold and shattered box office records.

But life at the top was tough for the duo. After five years they took a month's break at Christmas, Lennie going to his home, Di to her's in Hertfordshire.

They claimed they were both fed up of being away from home all the time.

Lennie once said of Di: "She really made our act. She's been my eyes on stage for many years."

Peters and Lee... an amicable parting.

Tracy Pidd (right) and friends

Bad wallpaper was all the rage

Making his view known on the state of the era

Living the life in 1980s Sheffield

DiRTY STOP OUT'S GUIDE to 1980s SHEFFIELD

photograph: Denis Lound.

11.4.86

Marcus Reynoulds at his Take Two studio at Staniforth Road, Attercliffe, Sheffield.

New live concert venue may open in July

by **DOM ROSKROW**

SHEFFIELD is to get a new live concert venue this summer.

And when the Take Two Music Club finally opens its doors around July, it will mark the end of the first chapter in a fairy tale success story.

For only last July Marcus Reynolds, the man behind the new venture, was granted a £40-a-week Government-backed enterprise allowance to get his business off the ground.

Since then the 35-year-old musician, who has been in the business for 22 years a sa session player has built up a rehearsal studio on Staniforth Road, Attercliffe.

By living off his wife's income, he has attracted bands like Floy Joy and Jimmy James & The Vagabonds to take advantage of the facilities. At the moment the rehearsal rooms are attracting more than 200 hours a month trade.

The new concert venue will be above the rehearsal rooms and will hold about 200 people. A provisional drinks licensek has been granted and Marcus hopes to hold rock, jazz and country nights.

"We've had record company interest in the place and everything's now getting really busy," said Marcus, who consulted among other jazz legend Ronnie Scott for advice.

"But we haven't got an exact opening date and we haven't planned the first night. It's a big risk."

Marcus believes he will be the first MSC person to become a club owner, and eventually hopes to expand with a recording studio. The present site will provide food, hire facitlities and a leisure area with pool table.

"A lot of people have commented about our site in Attercliffe but we are on a prime bus route and a sports centre is being built across the way," he said.

"I am very excited by the project because I want to give something back to the music business

ALL CONQUERING LEAGUE PAVES THE WAY FOR STEEL CITY CHART SUCCESS

There's no doubt the eighties belonged to the Human League.

They dominated the charts through the majority of the era with a sound and look that helped define the entire eighties generation.

The Phil Oakey-led synth act helped open the floodgates for the city's electro-pop movement that was already stirring around them and gave Sheffield a popular music scene that reverberated the world over.

The influence of the Human League's 1981 triple platinum 'Dare' album and multi-million selling 'Don't You Want Me' still resonates as strong today as it did as when it was first released.

Their sound was everywhere - school discos, youth clubs, supermarkets, nightclubs, over the airwaves. They broke Europe and the States.
The world was at their feet.

But it didn't start that way. The first incarnation of the band split acrimoniously in November 1980.

Music weekly Sounds said: "Their creative process had broken down, there was hardly any exchange of ideas within the band."

Insults were traded publicly and things got very messy but, incredibly, two bands appeared as a result and they both did far better than the one they were arguing about.

In fact the second Phil Oakey-led operation got that big he spent a lot of the 1980s holed up at home to avoid the attention and hassle he got.

But the Human League did perform some of their most legendary gigs in the city in the era.

They performed a two night sell-out stint at Sheffield Lyceum on Thursday and Friday, November 26 and 27, 1981, on the back of their triumph with 'Dare' released just weeks before. They also played five nights back-to-back at The Limit in 1986.

Phil Oakey actually had High Street's Crazy Daizy to thank for helping him to form Human League mark II - the reincarnation that set their fortunes into overdrive.

It was there he spotted two school girls - friends Joanne Catherall and Suzanne Sulley - who he enlisted for the band.

With absolutely no professional dancing or singing experience, they joined the group and remain part of the iconic act that works as hard today as it did then.

Success came thick and fast. Number ones on both sides of the Atlantic, awards and more.

But the Human League were only half of the Sheffield sound that was gaining airplay in their wake.

DiRTY STOP OUT'S GUIDE to 1980s SHEFFIELD

Artery

Below: Romeo & Juliet's started a night called Sound & Vision in June 1980 to try and emulate the success of the Crazy Daizy's Bowie night of the late seventies. This pic shows sisters (left to right) Margaret, Sylvia, Rita and Janet Fletcher with Tim

Heaven 17, formed out of the remains of Human League version one, were also massive.

Former Oakey sidekicks Martyn Ware and Ian Craig Marsh together with vocalist Glenn Gregory also enjoyed chart success for the majority of the era.

Named after a fictional band in cult film 'A Clockwork Orange', they were politically astute, cool and gave a further dimension to the city's influence on the country's music and fashion scene.

Their biggest single of the era was 'Temptation' which reached number 2 in the UK singles chart in 1983 but a raft of other hits like '(We Don't Need This) Fascist Groove Thing', 'Come Live With Me' and 'Crushed By The Wheels Of Industry' keep them in demand to this day.

Glossy and witty, ABC were formed out of the ashes of Vice Versa. The band successfully prised no less than four hit singles from debut album 'The Lexicon Of Love.'

They made their ABC debut at Psalter Lane Art College in September 1980. The audience were pretty gobsmacked by the band's total transformation from arty alternative to American funk with the image to go with it.

They were a near instant hit. Their second gig was at Penny's on Eyre Street - it was packed to the rafters.

It was a meteoric and well choreographed rise to the top. They were signed within months and in the top twenty with 'Tears Are Not Enough' by November 1981.

But it was 1982 that belonged to ABC. They shot down their cynics and eclipsed their rivals with three massive top ten hits that are still played on the radio as much as they ever were: 'Poison Arrow', 'The Look Of Love' and 'All Of My Heart'.

The subsequent album, 'The Lexicon Of Love', was a huge hit both here and in the States and stayed on the UK charts for a year.

Their gold lame suits became synonymous with eighties style and excess.

Though still years away from bothering the commercial charts, Jarvis Cocker's Pulp beavered away through the era with numerous line-up changes, numerous gigs and one extended stay in hospital.

Their defining moment of the era is regularly cited as Jarvis Cocker's re-emergence following a broken ankle, broken wrist and a fractured pelvis.

DiRTY STOP OUT'S GUIDE to 1980s SHEFFIELD

● The eighties were an incredibly productive time for Sheffield and its music

Pulp

He performed for the first time in a wheelchair at The Limit in January, 1986.

The enigmatic front man had decided to try and impress a girl with his Spiderman impression and managed to fall out of a Division Street first-floor flat in the process and land in front of Sven Books, a sex shop.

"It was senseless bravado", he quipped. "Which is quite out of character. I realised I didn't have the strength to do it, or to climb back in, so I had to count to three and let go."

The eighties were an incredibly productive time for Sheffield and its music.

Even Sheffield City Council got in on the act and unveiled their Red Tape Studios to help nurture talent and provide training for working in the music industry. It still runs today.

Other acts to make the headlines included Clock DVA, Comsat Angels, Cabaret Voltaire, The Stunt Kites, Mirror Crack'D, The Negatives, Artery, They Must Be Russians, Mau Maus, Artery and many, many more.

The Mirror Crack'd

DiRTY STOP OUT'S GUIDE to 1980s SHEFFIELD

Collecting for the Hillsborough Disaster Appeal

DiRTY STOP OUT'S GUIDE to 1980s SHEFFIELD

Three members of the future ABC

Looking towards Penny's

DiRTY STOP OUT'S GUIDE to 1980s SHEFFIELD

Baretta and passer-by

Echo And The Bunnymen at The Limit

LIMIT CLUB
WEST STREET : SHEFFIELD

Limit Club 5th Anniversary Night
ANIMAL NIGHTLIFE
THURSDAY, 24th MARCH, 1983

Half Price Admission with this Ticket

Rockerbilly rebels at The Limit

The Cramps at West Street's Limit

LIMIT'S LYCEUM GAMBLE BRINGS GIG HEAVEN TO SHEFFIELD

Another venue totally untouched by the early '80s recession was The Limit on West Street.

It was so successful that it was able to bankroll the transformation of Sheffield Lyceum from dilapidated eye-sore to state-of-the-art music venue and give it a grand unveiling as far back as 1981, years before it was converted back to a theatre.

The Limit, run by George Webster and Kevan Johnson, kicked off the Thatcherite-style decade of despondency in flamboyant style on Sunday, February 3, 1980. They hired out the nearby Top Rank on Arundel Gate and put the Ramones on. It was totally mental by all accounts.

Richard Malik:

"Though punk was well into its fourth year by then this gig must still rank as one of the best things I've ever seen or experienced. It was absolutely rammed.

"Me and a bunch of schoolmates came over on the train from Chesterfield. I remember various fights kicking off around Pond Street between the punks and trendies. It wasn't nice.

"I can still see Dee Dee Ramone bellowing '1234' into his mike even now, bless his soul.

"They came on in front of this blazing white bank of light and were met one of the biggest showers of gob I'd ever seen."

"It was hiring out the Top Rank that helped persuade the Limit management they could do one better and have their own venue capable of staging bigger shows.

The Sheffield Lyceum venture cost them dearly in terms of finances and the eventual breakdown of the original Limit partnership but even now, three decades after they unveiled the refurbed building, you have to take your hat off to what they achieved and the calibre of acts they promoted - it really was a who's who of early 1980s music and entertainment.

Their venture, which cost them an estimated £350,000 to revamp the Victorian theatre structure that had faced calls for demolition as far back as in the mid 1970s, brought groundbreaking shows to the city in the shape of The Clash, Simple Minds, U2, Spike Milligan and scores more.

It really was the mother of all venues for Sheffield. Fading Victorian opulence crossed with 20th century rock'n'roll - an incendiary combination.

The highlight for Lyceum co-owner George Webster was probably the homecoming shows for Sheffield legend Joe Cocker.

He originally booked him 19 years earlier when he was performing as Vance Arnold.

Above: Limit co-owner George Webster raises a glass to the reopening of Sheffield Lyceum (left)

Left: Joe Cocker performs at Sheffield Lyceum

DiRTY STOP OUT'S GUIDE to 1980s SHEFFIELD

● Nigel Lockwood

"Most people that went to The Limit would go boozing in the likes of nearby West Street bars like the Mailcoach, the Beehive, Hallamshire Hotel as well as the Grapes and Dog & Partridge on Trippet Lane.

"There'd also be the Victoria Wine Bar on West Street and Mr Kites wine bar on Devonshire Street.

"The Raven, which became the Hornblower in later years, was also popular as was the Foresters on Division Street together with the Three Tuns and The Museum around Leopold Street."

● Mick Dans

"The Lyceum was an awesome venue. I was gutted when it shut. I remember one freezing cold night - I think it was snowing - we went to see The Damned.

"I think the weather had put people off as there was hardly anyone there.

"I remember some old woman talking to us. She looked very out of place. It turned out to be front man Dave Vanian's mum!

"The Anti-Nowhere League supported them.

"It was the first time I heard 'So What' - what a song!"

The Selector at The Limit

DiRTY STOP OUT'S GUIDE to 1980s SHEFFIELD

● CLUB NIGHTS AT WEST STREET'S LIMIT

By the mid eighties The Limit was far better known for its club nights and gigs were becoming less frequent.

Limit DJ/manager Paul Unwin:
"Biggest problem we had as an organisation was that to get the good bands you had to take such a lot of rubbish, so a lot of the time we never made any money by putting on live acts.

"The disco was competing with the groups for popularity; owners George and Kevan soon realised that we could get people in the club on a Saturday night paying two pounds without having to pay an act."

For many Limit punters who were too young to catch the venue's early years, the club nights of the 1980s were as memorable as any band.

It became a true melting pot for punks, mods, Goths, indie kids, students and, especially on a weekend, football firms.

The bouncers became legendary for their ability to put down violence within seconds of it happening.

Arguably the worst incident was between visiting Leeds fans and the two local SUFC and SWFC firms.

The Limit's Steve Bolderson said: "There was a bunch of LUFC supporters who got a load of scaffolding poles from over the road and tried to ram the doors. We were stood behind them when the poles came flying through. It was as near as we came to a full scale riot: we just had to try and keep the doors locked."

The appearance of the Leeds fans was one of the few times the local firms of SWFC (named OCS) and SUFC (named BBC) joined together to do battle with a common enemy.

Working at The Limit, especially as security, definitely didn't come without its risks to life and limb.

Paul Unwin:
"We all used to train and keep fit because, when it did kick off, it really kicked off and could get nasty. I trained with a guy called Dave Cook who was a boxer."

The Limit held its own through the entire eighties era. Nothing seemed to dent its popularity.

Whilst overflowing toilets, sticky floors and mutterings of watered-down lager would signal the death knell for most venues, for The Limit it just seemed to work in its favour and the legend just gathered momentum.

Former Star writer and big Limit fan John Quinn said: "From the hazardous path down the stairs when entering the place (there were rumours of the existence of a lift, but no one I knew had ever seen it) to the sheer stickiness of the floors and the delightful decor (er, black), it wasn't the sort of place you'd want to take your parents unless you genuinely wanted them fearing for your sanity.

"And I'm not even mentioning the toilets.

"Because just thinking about them is bad enough."

● **"And I'm not even mentioning the toilets. "Because just thnking about them is bad enough."**

Limit regulars Laura Deeley and Allison Bowen

The Limit CLUB West Street
Tonight DISCO free before 10 p.m.
Tomorrow night DISCO free before 10 p.m.
Wednesday night REGGAE DISCO
Thursday night MATCHBOX
Tuesday, April 29 HOLLY & THE ITALIANS

● Phil Staniland

"The Stranglers did an infamous show at the Lyceum where there was a massive stage invasion of air guitar players. The band took it really well accommodating them for a song or two but got fed up when a few of the more drunk air guitarists wouldn't get off and one went up to bass player Jean Jacques Burnel and poured a full bottle of drink over his head (I think it may have been water). Not a good idea for two important reasons! Firstly the electrical factor - old JJ could have gone up in smoke and secondly JJ was a very high ranking karate expert!

"He was livid!! He stopped playing came up behind the kid and threw him in the audience.

"Everybody could sense it was going to happen but I can honestly say I have never seen anyone throw anybody as far ever! It was like tossing the caber.

"Another slightly unusual one was The Stray Cats at the Lyceum that I attended with support from (can you believe) Screaming Lord Sutch!"

TAKE ME TO the LIMIT — TEL 730940 WEST STREET SHEFFIELD

LYCEUM
LYCEUM THEATRE TUDOR WAY SHEFFIELD 1
PRESENTS
THE CLASH
Appearing on SUNDAY OCTOBER 11th
Price £3.50 DOORS OPEN AT 7 p.m. Stalls
Save this ticket for half price admission to the Limit Club, West Street. After this show, except weekends and special occasions.
Under 18's are only allowed in seated areas, except for special occasions No 658

Inside The Limit

WHATS ON IN OCTOBER AT THE LYCEUM
TUDOR WAY, SHEFFIELD 1

Under 18's Allowed in Seated Area.
Doors Open 7 p.m.

OPENING NIGHT
WEDNESDAY, 7th OCTOBER — Admission: £2.50, £3, £3.50
ODYSSEY

THURSDAY, 8th OCTOBER — Admission: £3 and £3.50
U2 and Special Guests

MONDAY, 19th OCTOBER — Admission: £3 and £3.50
GREG LAKE and Voyager
Gary Moore on Lead Guitar

FRIDAY, 23rd OCTOBER — Admission: £2.50 and £3
BAUHAUS and Wall of Voodoo

MONDAY, 26th OCTOBER — Admission: £2.50 and £3
BLUES BAND and Support

THURSDAY, 29th OCTOBER — Admission: £2 and £2.50
BOW WOW WOW and Support

FRIDAY, 30th OCTOBER — Admission: £3 and £3.50
GARY GLITTER and Support

SATURDAY, 31st OCTOBER — Admission: £2 and £2.50
Halloween Ball with THE GO GO'S From the U.S.A.

The Limit CLUB
70 WEST STREET, SHEFFIELD 1

Sunday Shows Membership Required 24 hours in Advance from LIMIT 50p.

SUNDAY, 4th OCTOBER — Admission: £1.50
REVILLOS and Support

THURSDAY, 8th OCTOBER — Admission: £1.50
GIRLS AT OUR BEST and Support
Half price admission with U2 ticket

SUNDAY, 11th OCTOBER — Admission: £1.50
THE PASSIONS and Support

THURSDAY, 15th OCTOBER — Admission: £1.50
DOLL BY DOLL and The Gas

TUESDAY, 20th OCTOBER — Admission: £2
CARLENE CARTER
Featuring Rockpile Members

THURSDAY, 22nd OCTOBER — Admission: £2
THEATRE OF HATE and Support

SUNDAY, 25th OCTOBER — Admission: £1.50
MARTIAN DANCE and Support

TUESDAY, 27th OCTOBER — Admission: £2
From the U.S.A.—Hit Single "Lawnchairs"
OUR DAUGHTERS WEDDING and Support

THURSDAY, 29th OCTOBER — Admission: £2
THE FALL and Support
Half price admission with BOW WOW WOW ticket

1st NOVEMBER — Admission: £1.50
THE SOUND and Local Support
Half price admission with GO GO'S ticket

In association with SOUTH YORKSHIRE COUNTY COUNCIL
PRESENT THURS SEPT 30th **CHELSEA** 7.30pm with THE METEORS + 1919
THEN OCT 4th **ANNIE ANXIETY CRASS, DIRT, SYSTEM + FLUX OF PINK INDIANS** + FILM - CHOOSING DEATH
PROMPT START 6.30pm
THURS OCT 7th **THE EXPLOITED** 8.00pm WITH THE MAU MAUS
ENTRANCE TO ALL GIGS 50p
AT THE LEADMILL, LEADMILL RD S1
PHONE 757500

THE UNDERTONES
IN CONCERT
PLUS SPECIAL GUEST

Nº 415

AT THE TOP RANK SUITE
ARUNDEL GATE, SHEFFIELD

wed 28th
on ~~SUNDAY, 25th~~ MAY, 1980

TICKETS in advance
DOORS OPEN 7.30 p.m.
LATE BAR

THE LIMIT CLUB
PRESENTS IN CONCERT
The Ramones
plus SUPPORT Band

Nº 1200

At the TOP RANK SUITE,
ARUNDEL GATE, SHEFFIELD.
ON SUNDAY 3rd FEB. 1980
Doors open 7.30 p.m.

Tickets £3.00 in advance

SUNDAY, 17th FEBRUARY, 1980
Derek Block Concert Promotions
presents
THE RUTS
PLUS SUPPORT

THE TOP RANK SUITE,
ARUNDEL GATE, SHEFFIELD, 1

TICKET £2.50 inc. VAT

Nº 0

OVER 18's ONLY

PRESENTS IN CONCERT
THE HUMAN LEAGUE
PLUS SPECIAL GUEST

_ 1764

AT THE TOP RANK SUITE
ARUNDEL GATE, SHEFFIELD

on TUESDAY, 20th MAY, 1980

TICKETS £2.25 in advance
DOORS OPEN 7.30 p.m.
LATE BAR

LYCEUM
TUDOR WAY, SHEFFIELD 1

Under 18's Allowed in Seated Area.
Doors Open 7 p.m.

WEDNESDAY, 11th NOVEMBER — Admission: £2 and £2.50
9 BELOW ZERO and The Check

THURSDAY, 12th NOVEMBER — Admission: £2.50 and £3
TENPOLE TUDOR and Support

SUNDAY, 15th NOVEMBER — Admission: £3 and £3.50
THE DAMNED and The Anti Nowhere League

TUESDAY, 24th NOVEMBER — Admission: £3 and £3.50
LINX and Support

WEDNESDAY, 25th NOVEMBER — Admission: £3 and £3.50
THE CURE and Support

THURSDAY, 26th NOVEMBER — Sold Out
THE HUMAN LEAGUE

FRIDAY, 27th NOVEMBER — Sold Out
SATURDAY, 28th NOVEMBER — Tickets on Sale now
THE STRANGLERS and Full Supporting Show

TUESDAY, 1st DECEMBER — Admission: £2.50
THE SLITS and Support

WEDNESDAY, 2nd DECEMBER — Admission: £3 and £3.50
HOT GOSSIP and Support

SATURDAY, 5th DECEMBER — Tickets on Sale now
ASWAD and Support

SUNDAY, 6th DECEMBER — Admission: £3.50
SLADE and Full Support

THURSDAY, 10th DECEMBER — Admission: £3
Australian Heavy Metal Band
"ROSE TATTOO"

SATURDAY, 12th DECEMBER — Admission: £3 and £3.50
SQEEZE and Support

NOVEMBER and DECEMBER AT THE LYCEUM

SUNDAY, 13th DECEMBER — All Tickets: £2.50
THE GOOD, THE BAD AND THE UGLY TOUR
with THE BUREAU, THE MO-DETTES,
RODDY RADIATION AND THE TEAR JERKERS

TUESDAY, 15th DECEMBER — Admission: £3 and £3.50
THE SUZI QUATRO SHOW

FRIDAY, 11th DECEMBER OR SUNDAY, 20th DECEMBER
HAWKWIND
(Check Press for Details)

Also Coming at Later Dates:
JUDIE TZUKE (2 Nights)
GRAHAM PARKER (2 Nights)

Advance tickets from Lyceum Box Office, Tudor Way, Sheffield.
Open 10 a.m.—3 p.m., Monday—Saturday. Enclose S.A.E. with Postal Applications. Telephone: 754944
Cheques payable to THERMABBE LIMITED.

The Limit CLUB
70 WEST STREET, SHEFFIELD 1

Sunday Shows Membership Required 24 hours in Advance from LIMIT 50p.

SUNDAY, 15th NOVEMBER — Admission at door
HEAVY METAL BAND
RAGE AND DFS / THE BADEY BROTHERS AND VIDEO'S
OF SAXON / AC/DC / FREE, ETC. / DOING ALRIGHT NOW

THURSDAY, 19th NOVEMBER — Admission at door
DAVID LINDLEY
(EX JACKSON BROWNE, ROLLING STONES, EAGLES, ETC.)

SUNDAY, 22nd NOVEMBER — Admission at door
THE CUBAN HEELS and Support

TUESDAY, 24th NOVEMBER
MISTY IN ROOTS and Support

THURSDAY, 26th NOVEMBER — Admission at door
HOT CUISINE and Support

SUNDAY, 29th NOVEMBER — Admission at door
A FLOCK OF SEAGULLS and Support

THURSDAY, 3rd DECEMBER — Admission at door
TV 21 and Support

THURSDAY, 10th DECEMBER — Admission at door
AFTER THE FIRE and Support

SUNDAY, 13th DECEMBER — Admission at door
WAY OF THE WEST and Support

THURSDAY, 17th DECEMBER — Admission at door
Q TIPS and Support

ROGER & OUT AND PUNK NIGHT AT THE MARPLES

Fitzalan Square's Marples venue was anarchy's Ground Zero in the heady days of the early eighties. The Sex Pistols might have imploded months earlier but there was an entire new generation of adrenalin-charged, guitar wielding carnage-merchants ready to fill their shoes.

The indie charts were awash with the doom-laden lyrics of Crass, Discharge, The Exploited, Conflict, Anti-Pasti, Sheffield's own Mau Maus and a legion of others and local promoter Marcus Featherby, a true Svengali figure who seemed to disappear from the scene as mysteriously has he arrived, lined the acts up week after week in the packed upstairs room in Sheffield.

There couldn't have been a more fitting place for the anti-war rallying cry of the bands and audiences, the original Marples Hotel was flattened by the Luftwaffe in 1940 and caused the biggest single loss of life in the Sheffield Blitz of World War Two.

Highlights of dole-charged years must have been Crass who had an ability to pack the place without having to do any advertising bar a bit of nicely stencilled graffiti in the odd subways; UK Subs fighting through the snow to get there with Sheffield's own Stunt Kites bringing up the rear with their own version of the nativity and the wanton carnage that was Discharge.

It's hard to know how so many mohawks, studs, DMs and towering spikey haircuts could fit in one room but they did.

The gigs had a true DIY feel and were a world apart from the bigger shows at Top Rank, Sheffield Poly, Sheffield City Hall and others.

Mark Brians:
"Punks would gather outside the Marples as early as the afternoon on gig night. The older, more intimidating ones would spend a bit of time begging change off the younger fans who'd obviously never been to a gig before - they were easy pickings. And then there was the hours spent queuing on the stairs to get in. It seemed to take forever."

But it wasn't just the punks that were entertained at the Marples; rock, indie, alternative - it all had its place. As punk went underground as the era moved on it had to downsize and ended up at places like George IV on Infirmary Road and other venues. Standing in the shadow of Kelvin Flats, George IV was also home to the Blitz club of the early 1980s that offered up the likes of I'm So Hollow, Comsat Angels, Richard Strange and others.

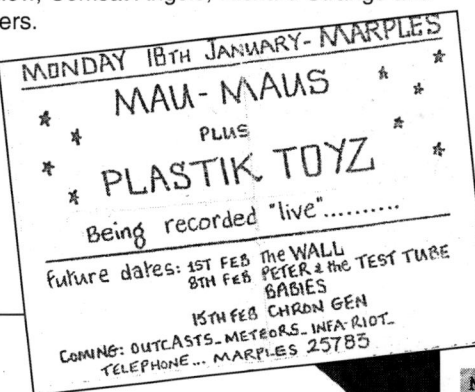

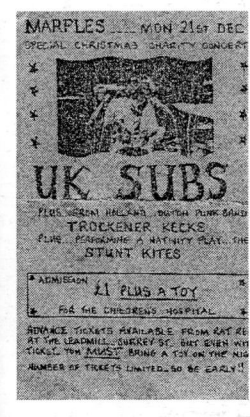

The Hole In The Road prior to falling into rack and ruin in the 1980s

DIRTY STOP OUT'S GUIDE to 1980s SHEFFIELD

● Diane Ridley: "I blame the Smurfs!"

"Well for me, the 1980s and the Sheffield music scene were synonymous but I might never have got into music were it not for the first single I was given - The Smurfing Song!

"Ahem! Eventually progressing to Adam and the Ants - by now about 13 years old and completely IN LOVE with Mr Goddard - I remember staring dreamily at the Top Rank knowing they had played there a few days earlier but alas, still too young to gig, that luxury was yet to come. Oh no, I had to be satisfied with waiting up for The Old Grey Whistle Test and hoping dad couldn't hear the little black and white portable in the bedroom or he'd go mad!

"Around the same time, many exciting bands were emerging from in and around Sheffield and coming from Chesterfield meant that if you wanted fun, shopping and generally a life, that was the place to go! It had to be Rebina for the boots (!) and it even had an 'oyl int middle ut rowed' which unless I'm very much mistaken, had some fish in an Aquarium - total sophistication to a Chezzy lass!

"Of course being so young, a visit to Sheffield usually involved delightful train journeys (past the sewage works) and on one occasion, I alighted onto the platform with Martin Fry from ABC - photo opportunity or what! My sister trumped that one though with her story of bumping into Joanne Catherall from The Human League in Debenhams who was buying a pair of socks for Phil Oakey - damn!!!

"Occasionally, Sheffield spilled over into Chesterfield and you got to experience the sound on your doorstep with bands like Vision appearing at the Aquarius (aka The Akka) - 'Lucifer's Friend' always filled the dance floor and reached the dizzy heights of number one, even if was only the Hallam charts (not even FM in those days!)!!!!

"Once we had done the electro sound, it was time to move onto something a bit more meaty - we were getting older and wanted something to get our teeth into which meant buying yards of PVC, running up mini skirts by the dozen ('You'll regret wearing that when you get older" Grandma said and she was right!), donning the fishnets and crimping Elnett infused bleached hair - oh and the longer you left it between washes meant it spiked up much better even if it did smell of stale fags!

"Think it must have been my older brother's fault - I remember him going to see The Stranglers (in Sheff of course!) way earlier and coming home with a T-shirt sporting a luminous rat - I had to have it! The wait wasn't too long - he needed to borrow my hair dryer - bingo!

"So, punk it was and groups of

Diane Ridley and fellow Chesterfield escapee

like-minded friends were evolving, mates started driving and collectively we were always looking for the next party and planning trips to the gigs - The Damned, UK Subs, Johnny Thunders, Anti-Nowhere League, Macc Lads, The Cult and umpteen bands we'd never heard of at the time (or since) - anything we could get to actually and life was sweet! The Gary Glitter gig in the mid '80s at the Top Rank was particularly good but you never hear him played on the radio these days do you?????

"The Leadmill became a regular haunt - (great because it wasn't far from the train station) and particularly good as you could nick the posters and stick them up in your bedroom when you got home - trophies like this were hard to come by in Chesterfield.

"I blame The Smurfs!"

Pickets at British Steel Corporation's Templeborough works

DiRTY STOP OUT'S GUIDE to 1980s SHEFFIELD

● SURVIVING A NIGHT AT THE FROG AND PARROTT

Unfeasibly strong real ale Roger & Out was probably about as near as Sheffield got towards a popularist after dark tourist attraction in the 1980s.

Sold in Devonshire Street's Frog & Parrott, it was treacle-like in texture and anaesthetic-like in taste - or at least that was the verdict from people that weren't real ale aficionados.

Sold in a third of a pint, you became the proud owner of a certificate after downing your first glass.

It proudly announced you'd now quaffed the strongest beer in the world according to the Guinness Book of Records.

The pub was massively popular amongst all comers.

Dave Jones:
"Roger & Out was absolutely vile but it had to be drunk. It was a matter of honour. I remember one of my mates had three glasses - the certificate presented for the third was deliberately blurred.

"It didn'it make any difference, my friend was virtually comatose by that point - but we had been drinking for an hour or two before that point.

"Other drinks I remember of the era were Pink Panthers - a kind of lager/cider/blackcurrant concoction - and the Red Witch, something similar and always guaranteed to ruin a carpet if the worst happened."

● Nigel Lockwood

"A lot of new wave acts had gone over ground by 1980 and started playing Sheffield City Hall. Bands like Secret Affair, the Pretenders and the Buzzcocks.

"The scene was beginning to get stale."

RatTrap

Ants
Bauhaus
Birthday Party
Cure
Cramps
Clash
Cabaret Voltaire
Cult
Doors
Damned
Echo and the bunnymen
Killing Joke

Lords of the new church
New Order
New York Dolls
Psychedelic Furs
Pil
Pogues
Siouxsie
Sisters of Mercy
Soft Cell
Spear of Destiny
Talking Heads
Velvets etc., etc., etc.,

★ every Friday night 9.30-2am
★ admission £1. (50p with this leaflet)
★ no restrictions on dress Before 10.30

VENUE
MONA LISA'S
Rockingham Street, behind Maximillions.

Home-based drinking prior to clubbing was a necessary evil in the cash strapped era

Government surplus became the clothing of choice for many

Quaffing homebrew at 'Dolebusters' - a match made in heaven

DiRTY STOP OUT'S GUIDE to 1980s SHEFFIELD

70

People's March For Jobs in Barker's Pool

```
CRASS - DIRT - ANNIE ANXIETY
Sunday 25th October 1981.
       at the Marples.
soft drinks only upstairs so
no age restrictions.
any profit will go to recording
costs for Wargasm - the antiwar
album on pax records, and the
Leadmill project.
Tickets printed by the
Sheffield Autonomous Anarchists
P.O.Box 168, Sheffield.
The 7 Modern sins: Apathy - Complacancy - Intolerance
Indifference - Ignorance - Blind Obedience - Divisions.
Don't let anyone lead you. Think for yourself. Have self
respect and respect others. Live your life the way YOU
want to and tolerate the way that other people want
to live theirs. Instead of fighting each other,
fight the systems which try to dominate and
control you. Anarchy = Peace and Freedom.
```

Pickets at Hadfields' East Hecla Works

DIRTY STOP OUT'S GUIDE to 1980s SHEFFIELD

REBINA AND X CLOTHES - HOW TO SIGN ON IN STYLE

CHAPTER TEN

X Clothes and Rebina Shoes really were Sheffield's fashion god and godess of eighties alternative fashion.

The former operation started in Leeds before opening its first Sheffield outlet on Leopold Street at the start of the era.

Punks, goths and rockers frequented it in their droves and it was the place to buy 'Crazy Colour' - the Day-Glo hair dye that no assuming alternative fashionista could ever be caught without.

The city's goth brigade had truly found their calling - they could now sign on in style.

Rebina Shoes, sited just off High Street, became a footwear institution for the entire region. Winkle pickers, brothel creepers, pointed buckle boots, patent leather, cool carrier bags - it could seemingly do no wrong. Just rack after rack after rack of the coolest shoes in the entire world.

They were Sheffield's Gucci of the dole-queue generation and the Internet message boards are full of Rebina threads to this day.

Susan Porter:
"I remember a girl turned up in some black leather pointed buckle boots to school which were obviously not Rebina. She was picked on mercilessly. If it wasn't Rebina it wasn't worth bothering with."

X Clothes ended up moving lock, stock and bullet belt to bigger premises directly facing the legendary Hole in the Road.

Unfortunately the once gleaming subterranean shopping precinct and pedestrian underpass that won a clutch of civic awards in its sixties and seventies infancy had now become little more than a magnet for arguing or comatose tramps and warring youth factions (especially at night).

The air of urban decay hung above it for the entire decade as the escalators packed up one by one and the graffiti artists gave it a makeover.

A sad era for a long gone inner city institution.

Left: Looking towards Barker's Pool

DiRTY STOP OUT'S GUIDE to 1980s SHEFFIELD

The fish tank, at least for younger sections of the community, was its crowning glory. Understated (it didn't even have signage) and slightly foreboding (it was all very dark and you always expected a monster from the deep to appear but it never quite did), kids were mesmerised.

It was one of the biggest tanks of its kind outside of London when it was first installed by all accounts.

The 1980s weren't such a good era for the fish. They were also caught up with the financial doom and gloom.

The late Kenneth Cornthwaite ended up coming to their rescue. He'd been concerned at the apparent disregard of the tank in the 1980s and wrote to the Town Hall.

Kenneth ended up looking after them personally. Under his watch there were around 19 fish including two rudd, two roach, three goldfish, two crusian carp, two bream, a chub, a dace, a golden rudd, an orfe, a tench and a koi carp.

He apparently fed them five times a week and they would regularly devour a pint of maggots and bread in two days.

If anyone knows their whereabouts these days we're all ears. There should be enough water in the new Peace Gardens to accommodate them somewhere.

● Jarvis Cocker

Jarvis Cocker, like many Sheffielders, remembers the Hole in the Road:

"The Hole in the Road also had a reputation for late night violence which made it a scary place to walk home through in the early hours - and this was not helped at all by the fact that the building's construction gave rise to an effect similar to that of the Whispering Gallery in St Paul's Cathedral - meaning that it was extremely difficult to work out where any menacing noises were coming from.

"Despite all this, the Hole in the Road was one of my favourite places in Sheffield and I would always show it to any out-of-town visitors.

"I was dismayed when it was knocked down and filled in, in the early '90s.

"When I go back to Sheffield and see the mini-roundabout that now occupies its space I always find myself thinking about the fish in the fish tank and what happened to them - or whether they're still down there in the dark; wondering where all the people have gone."

Queuing for cheap cigarettes on Orchard Street

DIRTY STOP OUT'S GUIDE to 1980s SHEFFIELD

● VINYL HEAVEN

Despite the recession and Miners' Strike, the 1980s were still a buoyant time for the record shops.

Even though half of Sheffield's music buying community seemed to be on the dole, traders could take solace in the fact that music ranked nearly as high as booze and cigarettes in the priority stakes - far higher than food and rent money obviously.

By the mid 1980s there actually seemed to be a proliferation in record shops in Sheffield as labels used everything from picture discs to a myriad of different record sleeves for each release as the perfect way to extract more cash from punters.

Rat Records majored on punk and hardcore and lived near The Leadmill; Castle Market's Revolution was punk and new wave Mecca; Bradley's seemed to be the place for chart and heavy metal; Virgin was hippy central but branched out in later years; Kenny's on the Wicker for rock'n'roll; Violet May for imports and rarities; Impulse for music and clothes on Cambridge Street which seemed to go on for about four miles and HMV for everything.

The list went on and on! These days there's little left bar Record Collector on Broomhill and Rare & Racy that still resides on Devonshire Street.

● Andrew Shawcroft

"Revolution Records was great but you always had to dodge the fights that always seemed to be kicking off on the Castle Market balcony every Saturday afternoon. It was far safer to go in the week I found."

● Glen Andrews

"I always wondered what happened to Rat Records - one day it was there, the next it was gone.
"Great carrier bags!"

Gateway supermarket, Buchanan Road, Parson Cross

DiRTY STOP OUT'S GUIDE to 1980s SHEFFIELD

74

Excelsior Inn on Carbrook Street

BRIAN'S SUMMER SENSATIONAL SALE
PEPE COTTON & CANVAS JEANS
£20 Now £9.99-£12.99
Ladies 8-16, Men's 28-36
Check — Plains. One-Off Bargains
£20-£20-£20-£20-£20

JEANS-JEANS-JEANS-JEANS

DAM YANKEE	SMAK (stone washed)
KAM-XPS £9.99 £11.99	£18 Now £10.99 Youths-Ladies-Men's £18-£18-£18-£18-£18
ICE-FROST £14.99 to £16.99	BIB 'n' BRACE £16.99 to £19.99
KIDS JEANS & Toddlers £4.99 XPS £7.99 Lee £8.99 Papa £14.99	TROUSERS Kids £4.99 Men's £9.99 COTTON SLACKS £14.99

SUMMER SHIRT SPECIAL

GALLINI Sweat shirts Were £13.99 Now £9.99	COLLARLESS Short Sleeve Shirts Were £9.99 Now £5.99
SPORT SHIRTS Men's & Boys 28in.-44in. chest £3.99	Short Sleeve Shirts 2 for £9 Checks-plain-stripes

SUMMER STOCK FOR THE BIG MAN
Sports Shirts to 56in. chest £5.9
JACKETS 60in. chest from £13.
SLIP OVERS to 56in. chest £4.

HARRINGTONS CASTLE MARKET Tel. 22694

HENRY'S Cafe Bar & Restaurant
SHOPPERS LUNCH
SERVED 12.00-2.30 p.m.
MONDAY TO SATURDAY
2 COURSE LUNCH INCLUDING COFFEE & MINTS
£3.50 INC. V.A.T.
FOR FULL DETAILS PHONE HENRY'S
Henry's Cafe Bar and Restaurant, Cambridge Street, Sheffield S1 4HP. Tel. 752242

Alpha HOTEL

DINING OUT IN SHEFFIELD
There's one Restaurant that stands out from all the rest.
Visit the Beauchief for a combination of comfort, hospitality and excellent cuisine.
CHRISTMAS FAYRE
SPECIAL DISCOUNT PRICE
LAST WEEK NOVEMBER
FIRST WEEK DECEMBER
4 COURSE MEAL WITH COFFEE & MINTS
FULL CHOICE OF MENU
£10.00 INCLUDING SERVICE CHARGE & V.A.T.
Telephone
The Beauchief
The Beauchief Restaurant
161 Abbeydale Road South, Sheffield S7 2QS
Tel. (0742) 360601

JEEVES AUTUMN SPECIAL
EVERY FRIDAY & SATURDAY UNTIL NOVEMBER 23rd
3-COURSE DINNER £13 for 2 inc. of V.A.T.
SUNDAY LUNCH
ROYAL VICTORIA HOTEL
VICTORIA STATION ROAD, SHEFFIELD 758227

Dining out...in Town
TUCKWOODS
EVENING MEALS
Waitress served first class Traditional Meals.
Table d'Hote or a la Carte Menus
The perfect place for Dining Out in Town.
Last Orders Monday to Thursday: 10.30 p.m.
Friday and Saturday 11 p.m.
SURREY STREET
(Top of Fargate)

Packing department at Richardson's and proof there were people in employment

DiRTY STOP OUT'S GUIDE to 1980s SHEFFIELD

PAULA YATES FAILS TO PULL AT RADIO RENTALS

The 1980s, like any other era, had more than its fair share of off the wall moments. Nigel Lockwood seemed to have the knack of being at the centre of all of them. He was one of about three people that turned up to witness Paula Yates doing the honours of opening a new Radio Rentals shop on Fargate.

The then Tube presenter might have been at the top of her game but it obviously didn't wash with Sheffield that morning. "Nobody turned up!", said Nigel Lockwood.

One fading star actually had more joy in Sheffield than many other places. Gary Glitter played a headline gig at the Top Rank in 1984 as part of 10th birthday celebrations for Radio Hallam - tickets were a mere £1 for anyone that could produce a UB40 and the crowd seemed full of punks and anyone else that would ordinarily give him a wide berth.

Stranger still was a personal appearance in Millhouses Park for Radio Hallam again.

Recession normally seems to go hand in hand with a proliferation in low brow amusement arcades offering cups of tea at 5p and other stunts to make a hole in the nearest Giro.

One opened in Woodseats in the era. Liz Dawn aka Coronation Street's Vera Duckworth (with a little help from Nigel Lockwood) did the opening honours.

Paula Yates opens the new Radio Rentals "Superstore" Saturday, 11th October, 11.00am - Radio Rentals Limited 53/55 Fargate Sheffield Yorks S1 2HD (0742) 755740

Liz Dawn opens a Woodseats amusement arcade with help from Nigel Lockwood

3266 GARY GLITTER THE INTERNATIONALS Top Rank Suite 1st OCT 1984 Tickets £1(UB40 holders)

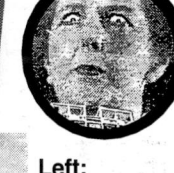

Left: Gary Glitter at Millhouses Park with DJ Ray Stuart (left) in 1981

Angel Street's ABC Cinema

CHAPTER ELEVEN

DiRTY STOP OUT'S.COM

DiRTY STOP OUT'S GUIDE to 1980s SHEFFIELD

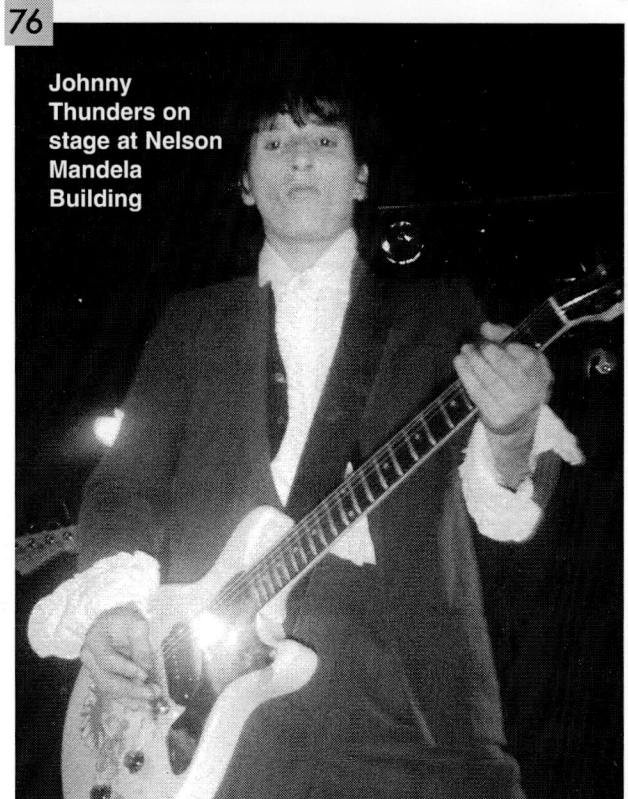

Johnny Thunders on stage at Nelson Mandela Building

Big Audio Dynamite make their live debut at The Leadmill

Keith Skues interviews Ade Edmondson at the opening of Crystal Peaks Cineplex in May 1988

The Housemartins at The Leadmill

Sigue Sigue Sputnik in Sheffield

DiRTY STOP OUT'S GUIDE to 1980s SHEFFIELD

The satirical puppets of Spitting Image were a hit the minute they first hit the screen in 1984.

They also turned up at The Leadmill - one either side of Nigel Lockwood who'd just won a holiday

The opening of a shiny new HMV outlet on Pinstone Street in July 1982 was a busy affair.

The two-storey operation was opened by none other than Dexy's Midnight Runners who were knee deep in their 'Come On Eileen' phase.

That was the same year that the Mulberry Tavern unveiled reputably the city's first video jukebox.

Cinemas were having a lean time in the 1980s. Video cassette players were on the rise and the big screen was all but being written off.

But then, in May 1988, everything changed with the arrival of the city's first multi-plex at Crystal Peaks.

Cinemas were once again cool and in demand.

Ade Edmondson and Barbara Windsor, amongst others (including Nigel Lockwood), attended the unveiling.

Above:
Kevin Rowland of Dexys Midnight Runners signs autographs at the opening of HMV on Pinstone Street in July 1982

Left:
Nigel Lockwood wins a holiday voucher at The Leadmill

Below:
Rex Cinema, junction of Mansfield Road and Hollybank Road, Intake

MEETING OUTSIDE THE FISHTANK IN THE HOLE IN THE ROAD

Julie Roche:
"I was in the prime of my life in the 1980s, celebrating my 21st birthday in 1982. To this day I still go into Sheffield with the same friends as I did then and we still talk of our nights out and what fun we had.

"My earliest memory of nightlife in Sheffield was going to the Fiesta nightclub (next to The Roxy) and seeing a group called the Dooleys. This was a trip from where I used to work at Thos W. Wards in the Wicker, Sheffield. We had a fantastic social life at Tommy Wards as we called it and because of the huge amount of young people who worked there we always had something to celebrate (usually some night out every week).

"We used to do a pub crawl every Christmas Eve up the Wicker at lunchtime when we finished work. Starting off at the Hole In The Wall, The Station Hotel and then working our way up to Sheffield town centre. We started at 12-ish and by 3.00 pm were usually finished and on the bus on our way home!!

"Another early memory is meeting my friends on a Friday/Saturday night at the fish tank in the Hole In The Road (now filled in) near to where Primark is now located.

"This was probably the most popular meeting place in Sheffield centre. From there we use to do a pub crawl as follows:- Mulberry Tavern (Arundel Gate), The Claymore, Dove and Rainbow, Wig and Pen (Campo Lane), Golden Ball then finishing off at the Stonehouse. Later on in the '80s my friends and I use to meet at a pub called Legends on High Street (formerly the Crazy Daizy) which was a popular pub - no upstairs you went downstairs to the large bar area. I always remember the Michael Jackson song and video ('Thriller') being played in there on its release. I can see me and my friends now watching it and dancing whilst drinking our favourite drink of dry cider and blackcurrant!. After our pub crawl we then went on to Romeo and Juliet's on Bank Street for a good old boogie (big music of the time was from the Bee Gees - Saturday night Fever film). I always remember basket meals of burger and chips being served there. If we didn't always manage a basket meal we would head to a mobile catering van in Fitzalan Square for a chip butty or burger before queuing for our black cab home.

"The big nightclub that took over from Romeo and Juliet's was Steelys nightclub on Arundel Gate (which then became Roxys) - what brilliant music was played there - Soft Cell ('Tainted Love'), Adam and the Ants ('Ant Music'), Orchestral Manoeuvres in the Dark ('Maid of Orleans') to name a few. It was an absolutely brilliant, thriving nightclub with a huge dance floor. I still see couples who met in there and have stayed together.

"If we wanted to have a change of pubs/route we sometimes use to meet in The Cannon (near Castle Market) then go to the Hen and Chickens (opposite) then go to the Museum pub and Brown Bear (near the Town Hall) and then to the Surrey Pub (with The Fringe on top - which was a gym above the pub).

"Another popular place in the 1980s was a nightclub called Fannys at Owler Bar on the way to Foxhouse in Derbyshire - we use to book a coach (usually for a special birthday - 18th or 21st) and have a night out there. It had a bar with a large dance floor.

"Later on in the 1980s we tried some different (in some cases) refurbished pubs, namely the Pig and Whistle (Leopold Street), Red Lion (back of the City Hall), The Saddle (West Street) before venturing into the famous Josephine's nightclub. I remember queuing to get in there

Julie Roche and friends at the Mulberry Tavern

and when queuing you could look through the tinted windows and see who was in the 'wine bar' area. I know of so many people who met in Josephine's and went on to get married, including my sister. The songs we danced to was Lionel Richie ('Dancing on the Ceiling'), Billy Ocean ('When The Going Gets Tough'), Kylie Minogue ('I Should Be So Lucky')- incidentally my best friend was Kylie's double but unfortunately like me as the years pass the pounds have piled on!!, Rick Astley ('Never Gonna Give You Up') and then of course the smoochies - the most popular one I remember was 'Lady' by Lionel Richie.

"If me and my friends felt like a change of scenery we would sometimes venture down London Road in Sheffield: the Tramway, Barrel, Crown Inn being the most popular.

"Every Saturday afternoon me and friends went to Sherbet gym on The Moor (most popular gym in Sheffield in the '80s), originally owned by Marti Caine. Where we use to do our aerobic classes. then we use to shower, put our makeup on then head to the shops to buy a new outfit for our Saturday night. Our favourite clothes shops were Wallis, Principles and Chelsea Girl and Debenhams. Then we use to head off home, eat then get glammed up for our 'big' Saturday night out. Sunday afternoons were spent swimming off our hangovers at the now demolished Sheaf Valley Baths in Pond Street and planning our pub route for the following weekend!!

"I also recall going to see the Human League in the '80s at the Lyceum Theatre in Sheffield - they were brilliant.

"Our favourite eating places in the '80s were:
The Wimpy (for burger), 4 Seasons Restaurant (on Arundel Gate), Uncle Sams (Ecclesall Road) the Coach House (steak house in the Wicker) Zing Vaa (The Moor) and of course burger and chips in Romeo and Juliet's."

The Museum on Orchard Street

JIVE TURKEY- THE COOLEST CLUB IN THE COUNTRY?

By the mid eighties a new breed of night culture was making initial waves in key cities across the UK - a scene that would eventually change the face of nightlife forever and turn Sheffield into one of the UK's dance-led club land capitals by 1995.

House music had been evolving in the likes of New York and Chicago since the early eighties.

Sheffield, buoyed on by Manchester's Hacienda which was soon to throw itself in hook, line and ecstasy tablet in to the scene, was one of the earliest adopters of the burgeoning dance movement in the UK.

Though the city didn't have a dedicated dance club in the late eighties, various nights were starting to appear like the Wednesday night Steamer at The Leadmill; the monthly Jive Turkey at Sheffield City Hall Ballroom and more regular offerings at Mona Lisa's (which had become Occasions by the late 1980s).

DJ Parrot and musical sidekick Winston Hazel were two of the scene's true originators in the city and were seen as largely responsible for introducing house and techno to Sheffield and the region.

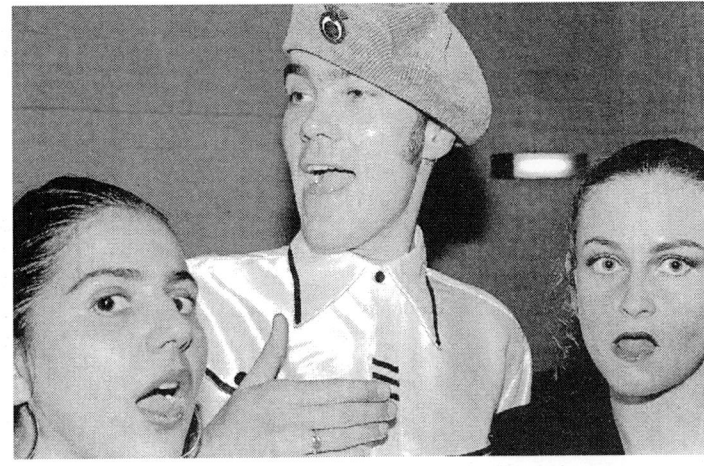

They were behind Jive Turkey and many of the events at Occasions like Club Superman.

Parrot, fed up with the scene at the likes of The Leadmill and The Limit, decided to do his own thing around 1985 and ended up DJing by default because he owned more records than any of his friends when they came to starting their own night.

By 1988 Jive Turkey was attracting coach loads from around the region and further. The Observer featured it in November that year. They said:

"Inside, local dance entrepreneurs Jive Turkey offer the perfect antidote to Sheffield's brusque and rough nightlife.

"With the co-operation of the socialist city council, the trio of Matt, John and Parrot provide a relentless pulse of funk, jazz and house rhythms finely attuned to Sheffield's black-music-loving, fashion conscious coterie.

"It is the city's obsession with contemporary dance styles, especially House, that creates such a heady ambience at the monthly Jive Turkey night. Records like 'Check This Out' by Hard House, 'Voodoo Ray' by A Guy Called Gerald and 'Hip Hop Salsa' by Bad Boy Orchestra - the latest nom-de-danse of House guru Todd Terry - produce a mesmeric weave over and around the dance floor.

"The crowd is mixed, with local blacks in flying jackets and Davy Crockett caps dancing next to young whites in Levis and short razored hair.

"This month, however, the influence of acid house is inescapable.

"The whole style kit is here: knotted hankies, shorts, polka-dot shirts, and a smile inane enough to frighten even the most zealous moonie."

Top and left: Acid house arrives in Sheffield

DiRTY STOP OUT'S GUIDE to 1980s SHEFFIELD

London Road

Mr Kite's Wine Bar on Devonshire Street

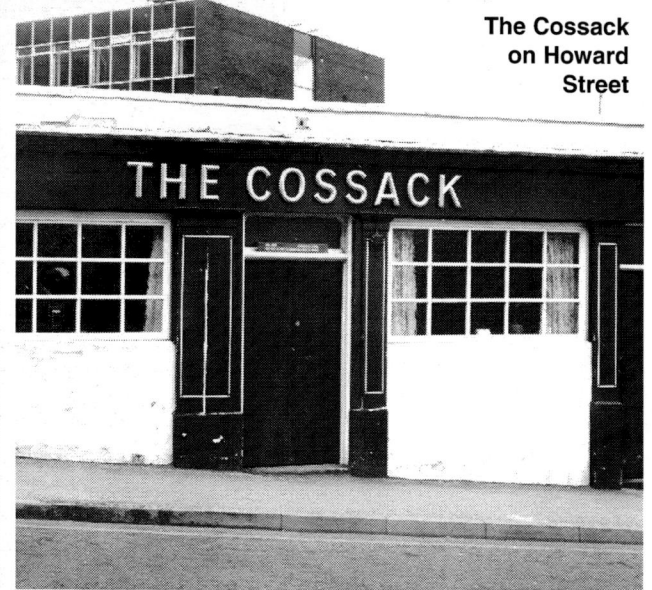

The Cossack on Howard Street

● Lindsay McLaren

"I remember going to The Steamer at the Leadmill when I was about 17/18. I didn't know anything about the night, other than I was going for a night out with a friend from school who had a cool boyfriend (he lived in Sheffield while we were stuck in Rotherham, he was over 20, knew the cool clubs and owned a car).

"We walked into The Leadmill and I fell in love with the atmosphere straight away. Smoky, dark, and not a badly fitted Burtons suit in sight. It was just jeans and t shirts, a thumping bassline and a mass of sweaty bodies.

"People were there for the music, not out on the pull.

"So different than the clubs my friends had dragged me to in the past where their definition of a good night was getting a snog off some random bloke on the dance floor.

"I was already into different music to my friends of the time, but I had never been to a club that played it until The Steamer.

"It kick-started a very long and hedonistic period of clubbing at venues throughout the country (and Ibiza of course). The DJ on the night was Graeme Park, and more than 20 years later, his name on the DJ line-up is enough to encourage me and the girls to head out to a club even now."

Looking up The Moor

DiRTY STOP OUT'S GUIDE to 1980s SHEFFIELD

Some of the earliest dance hits came from Sheffield as well.

DJ Parrot was one part of dance music studio-based act The Funky Worm that recorded at renowned Sheffield studio of the era, FON. It was formed by Mark Brayden - who went on to form Moloko in the mid 1990s - with Julie Stewart on vocal duties.

Their 'Hustle! (To The Music)' reached number 13 in the UK singles chart and was a massive club hit in 1988.

The year before saw the release of Krush's 'House Arrest' - a pioneering example of early UK house. It was produced by Mark Brydon and Warp Records co-founder Rob Mitchell.

Sheffield's Warp Records become one of the earliest and most influential dance labels of the time.

Launched in 1989 by Steve Beckett, Rob Mitchell and Robert Gordon, their first release (WAP1) was by Forgemasters.

● Paul Barnes

"I remember Saturday afternoon break dancing sessions at The Limit - they were ace! There'd be break dance challenges on Fargate and outside Roxy."

● Julie Shaw

"We thought we were the coolest people on the planet at Jive Turkey. And considering what else was going on Sheffield at that time we probably were!

"Drugs weren't really a part of the scene at that point - it was very much about the music and the fashions.

"We couldn't believe we'd been let loose in the splendour of the City Hall Ballroom. It was amazing.

"Even standing in the queue was a fashion statement amongst all the other really cool people.

"Sheffield hadn't seen anything like it.

"There was an incredible racial mix as well. People would come from all over the country."

The limited 500 copy pressing of 'Track With No Name' was financed by an Enterprise Allowance grant and distributed in a borrowed car. It set a trend for the early releases both in terms of sound, and the use of purple sleeves designed by the city's own Designers Republic.

The follow-up was Nightmares on Wax's 'Dextrous', which sold around 30,000 copies.

The influence of Sheffield's own Cabaret Voltaire can't be forgotten. Formed as far back as 1973, they gained acceptance with the arrival of punk but it was their pioneering of experimental dance and singles like 'Sensoria' that saw them appealing to a whole new audience in underground dance clubs in the 1980s and 1990s.

Whilst Sheffield provided the electro-pop of the early eighties, Manchester returned the favour with Madchester and its up-for-it stable of carnage-merchants comprising the likes of Happy Mondays, Stone Roses, 808 State that came through at the latter half of the eighties.

Part retro, part hippy, part football casual and but full on 24/7 party - baggy was in, smiley faces were everywhere and the world didn't know quite what to make of things.

Below: Fit for clubbing - the Josephine's All Stars

Top of Fargate

DiRTY STOP OUT'S GUIDE to 1980s SHEFFIELD

The author

Neil Anderson

Neil Anderson first launched Sheffield's 'Dirty Stop Out's Guide' in 1994 as a no-holds barred insight into the city's after dark scene.

He went retro with the 'Dirty Stop Out's Guide To 1970s Sheffield' in 2010 and followed that, more recently, with a 1960s version.

The 1980s were the era when he first hit after dark Sheffield in person at the likes of The Limit, The Leadmill, Rebels, the Marples, Dingwalls and other dens of iniquity.

Neil has written on nightlife and entertainment for titles spanning The Independent to The Big Issue and was a Sheffield Telegraph columnist for 12 years.

When he's not writing books about nightlife venues he's busy promoting them and other businesses through his All Credit Media communications agency www.allcreditmedia.com

Acknowledgements

Sheffield Newspapers for use of their wonderful pics and articles, Sheffield Local Studies Library for help digging out articles and pics, Sheffield City Council, Dave Manvell, Garry Wilson, Peter McNerney, Rachel Mellor, Nigel Renshaw, Olga Marshall, Paul Unwin, Pete Gill, Clive Porter, Andy Smith, Phil Staniland, Julie Wilson, Dave Allen, Julie Batty, Rachael Hope, Pete Hill for the fab photos, Martin Bedford for the great Leadmill posters, Tony Beesley, Mary Givens, Geoffrey Beattie, Steve Stevlor, Chris Walker, Nigel Lockwood and a memorabilia collection that, in fairness, probably surpasses Ohio's Rock and Roll Hall of Fame, Caroline Gowing, the girls at The Star Shop, Marcus Reynolds, John Quinn, Lez Wright, the Bailey Brothers, Steve Baxendale, Glenn Marples, Terry Davies, Haydn Anderson, Ken Hall, Ainsley Stones, Mick Shakespeare, Colin Drury, Matt Monfredi, Jane Salt, Real Radio, Karl Lang, Mark Hobson, Julie Roche, Diane Ridley, Shaun Stevenson, Rita Collins and Tracy Pidd.

Interview transcribing, proofing and all round inspiration: Lindsay McLaren.

Photography, proofing and balancing the books: Ian Cheetham.

Proofing: Peter Eales.

Mail order: Karen Davies.

Reality checks: Lowri and Ewan Anderson

The Dirty Stop Out's Guide trademark is owned by Neil Anderson and licensed to ACM Retro Ltd.

★ACM RETRO

BIG SISTER IS WATCHING YOU

1984

One of many era-defining posters by Leadmill artist Martin Bedford

DiRTY STOP OUT'S GUIDE to 1980s SHEFFIELD

★ ALSO AVAILABLE FROM ★ACM ЯETRO www.acmretro.com

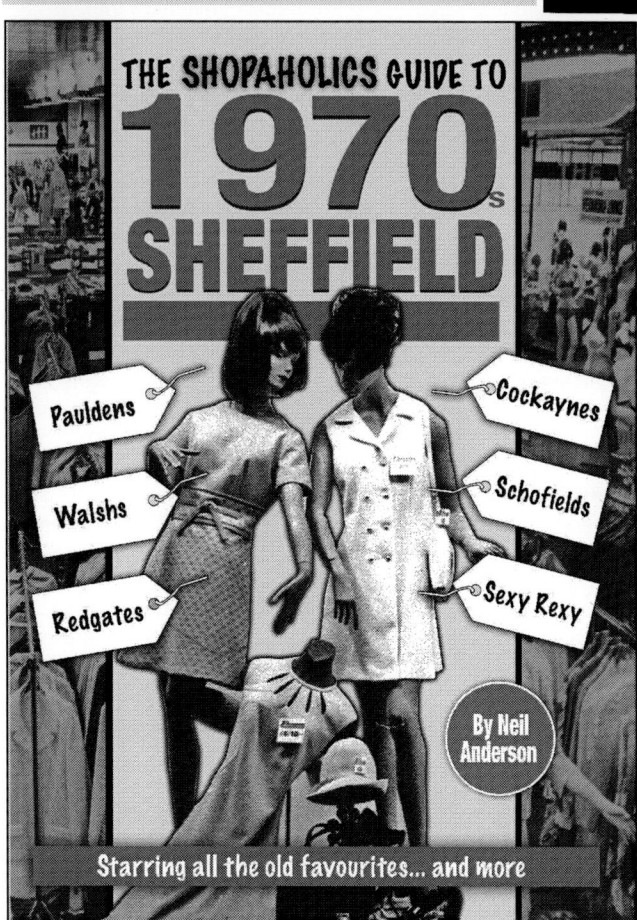

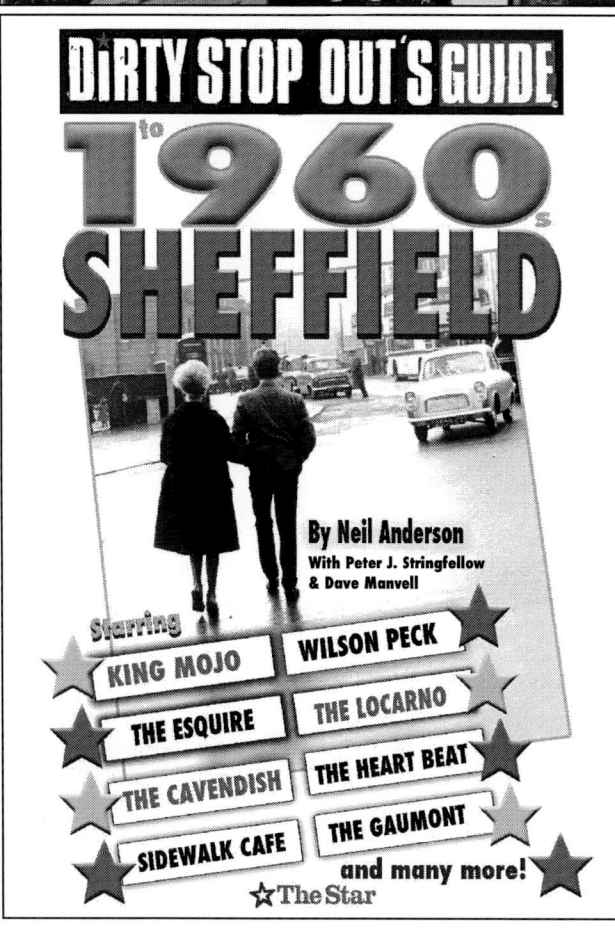

THE SHOPAHOLICS GUIDE TO 1970s SHEFFIELD
By Neil Anderson

- Pauldens
- Walshs
- Redgates
- Cockaynes
- Schofields
- Sexy Rexy

Starring all the old favourites... and more

DiRTY STOP OUT'S GUIDE to 1970s SHEFFIELD
By Neil Anderson

Starring:
- CLUB FIESTA
- CRAZY DAIZY
- PENNY FARTHING
- HOFBRAUHAUS
- BUCCANEER
- JOSEPHINE'S
- PENTHOUSE
- TOP RANK

and many more!

☆ The Star

DiRTY STOP OUT'S GUIDE to 1960s SHEFFIELD
By Neil Anderson
With Peter J. Stringfellow & Dave Manvell

Starring:
- KING MOJO
- WILSON PECK
- THE ESQUIRE
- THE LOCARNO
- THE CAVENDISH
- THE HEART BEAT
- SIDEWALK CAFE
- THE GAUMONT

and many more!
☆ The Star

SIGNING ON FOR THE DEVIL
SHEFFIELD - METAL CAPITAL OF THE 1980s
by Neil Anderson